BATTLEFIELD

SYSTEMS

INTEGRATION

Major General Ira A. Hunt, Jr.,
USA (Ret.)

PREFACE

This book depicts the actions taken post-Vietnam by the US Army to successfully combat a potential Soviet aggression in Europe. Today, after a decade of concentrating on counter-insurgency operations, the US Army finds itself with many newly developed combat systems that have not been fully integrated as a coherent force. The same situation existed in 1975 when the Office of Battlefield System Integration (BSI) was established to look at the Army's weapons systems in the context of a total system and to determine the Army's most effective battlefield systems. It is believed that the analyses taken then could be of value today.

BSI thoroughly analyzed enemy (Soviets) military capabilities and by utilizing heterogeneous dynamic modeling determined the relative value of one combat system to others so that meaningful trade-offs between systems could be made and a balanced US force designed.

Combat power, a function of weapons lethality and the number of engaged combatants, can be increased both through weapons enhancements and force multipliers. Force multiplication is the friendly increase or enemy decrease of engaged weapons and depends greatly on intelligence, surveillance and target acquisition as well as effective command and control. Force multiplication is powerful and victory often depends upon it!

MG Ira A. Hunt Jr. (Ret.)

TABLE OF CONTENTS

TABLES

MAPS

CHARTS

MG Ira A. Hunt Jr. (Ret.)

INTRODUCTION

In 1975, the US Army was required to refocus its attention from the counter-insurgency in Southeast Asia to a potential all-out major conflict in Europe. After a decade of concentrating on fighting counter-insurgency, the Army found itself with many newly-developed combat systems that had not been fully integrated into a cohesive force. Not only that, the Army was undergoing the largest modernization program in its history (developing the Abrams tank, the Bradley infantry fighting vehicle, a myriad of sensor systems, and new command and control systems, among others), attempting to play catch-up with the modernized Soviet military force that posed a threat to NATO in Central Europe. At that time the Office of Battlefield Systems Integration (BSI) was established to look at the Army's weapons systems in the context of a total system in order to integrate existing systems and to exploit opportunities offered by advancing technologies.

The situation today, after a decade of conflict in the Middle-East, is similar but more daunting because the Army finds itself with aging and worn-out equipment and a legacy of recent procurement programs in disarray. Today the Army is undergoing a "Transformation", shifting from threat-based planning to capability-based planning, with the goal of spreading the Army capabilities across a spectrum of potential threats. The transformed Army will be lighter and more capable of rapid deployment to the future hot spots of the world. Responsiveness, flexibility, and interconnect ability are the current buzz words. One thing is obvious, not only equipment but organizations, force structure, and training will also have to undergo a transformation.

BSI adopted a battlefield architecture which was an evolutionary plan synchronizing the development of doctrine, forces, materiel, and technology in order to forecast technological advances leading to potentially new systems which are required to be integrated while at the same time determining optimum numbers and types of systems within given cost parameters which should exist on the battlefield. The architecture was simply a matrix of nine mission areas mirroring "How the Army Fights" and thirty-nine functional groups of systems encompassing all 500 existing army systems. As a first step we then related technological progress to battlefield systems thereby prioritizing requirements. By focusing on operational capability requirements we were able to determine the pacing problems preventing developments and the work units necessary to solve the problems. The interface between developers and users is important since we found twenty-three percent of active developmental programs at the time had no specific user interest.

Next, to answer the question "Where is our money going?" we utilized a unique closed system input-output analysis of equipment life-cycle costs. Although decision makers generally focus on non-recurring investment costs we found that initial procurement costs were only eight percent of the twenty year life-cycle cost of a typical corps. Military personnel absorbed fifty percent of the twenty year costs and Supply and Transportation was by far the most costly fundamental group.

The equipment challenge of "What do we need?" and "What can we afford?" is a function of both costs and combat effectiveness. Therefore, a thorough analysis of the capabilities of potential enemies is necessary to determine combat effectiveness. The relative value of one combat system to another requires dynamic modeling to consider meaningful trade-offs between systems. All actions on the battlefield, both friendly and enemy, are interactive and all changes have a rippling effect. For example, if the improved armor on the Abrams tank greatly reduces the lethality of enemy ATGMs, then the value of enemy ATGMs is also greatly reduced as well as the value of friendly weapons that kill enemy ATGM's.

Combat power, a function of weapons lethality/survivability and the number of engaged combatants, can be increased both through weapons enhancements and force multipliers. Force multiplication in a battle is the friendly increase or enemy decrease of engaged weapons and depends greatly on intelligence, surveillance and target acquisition as well as effective command and control. Force multiplication is powerful.

Success on the battlefield depends greatly upon the proficiency and spirit of soldiers. The man-machine interface is very important. In the mid-seventies, as today, manpower skills were not improving but weapons were greatly increasing in complexity and the army was faced with the requirement to procure advanced weapon systems which would be more difficult to operate and maintain. The man-machine interface can only be solved by giving special attention to the training and schooling of soldiers to include training materials. Performance must be hands on and task oriented to improve the proficiency of soldiers. Today the army's soldiers, like their equipment, are worn-out by multiple assignments to combat areas.

Throughout the centuries the conduct of warfare has inexorably evolved in complexity and intensity. As the military power of nations has increased so have the economic and human costs. Success on the battlefield depends upon three major variables: the capabilities of weapons, the proficiency and spirit of soldiers, and the tactics and techniques of the commanders. In other words, the strategic and tactical capabilities of military leaders are a function of the organization and equipment available, and transcendently upon the training and spirit of their soldiers to effectively operate the equipment and to maneuver as required. As a background to discussing the integration of the modern battlefield, a cursory review of the changing characteristics of warfare is deemed necessary.

Hannibal, (247-183 BC)[1], the Carthaginian general in the Second Punic War between Carthage and Rome in 218 BC, led his Army of some 50,000 men from his base in Spain into Italy, crossing the Alps in mid-winter. Hannibal's goal, nurtured by a strong hatred of Rome, was to destroy the Roman Army. In order to draw the Romans to battle he moved his troops to the vicinity of Cannae in the south of Italy, an area which at the time was the lush granary of the Empire. Astride their food source, the Romans were forced to attack him. When the 72,000 men in the legions of Rome attacked, Hannibal had his center fall back. The Romans, sensing victory, rushed to press their perceived advantage. On order, Hannibal's center, now concave, stood its ground while the Carthaginian flank units enveloped the Romans, closing the trap. It is estimated that over 50,000 Romans were slaughtered that day. This double envelopment was the classic battle of annihilation and an outstanding example of a defensive-offensive maneuver. It was the result of careful planning and execution. The tactics and techniques of commanders is often transcendent.

The infantry of those times fought with handheld weapons and for over a thousand years weaponry was not dramatically improved. Weapon's effectiveness depended primarily on the dexterity of the individual. The battle of Crécy[2], which took place in northern France on 26 August 1364 between Edward III of England and Philip VI of France, was a transitional battle noted for the English use of the longbow and the introduction of cannon, probably for the first time in battle. Edward chose a defensive position along a mile-long ridge which faced downward sloping, open ground. The mounted French knights were spoiling for a battle, and that afternoon they immediately engaged in an uncoordinated attack. Once the battle was joined, the French kept attacking with at least a dozen mounted charges only to be driven off. The French, suffering heavy losses, withdrew at nightfall. Edward's choice of defensive terrain and his formations were exemplary, whereas Philip's lack of control of his knights and their continual, uncoordinated attacks indicated again the importance of leadership on the battlefield. Edward's longbow was formidable in direct fire, but a hail of arrows in indirect fire was also effective in slowing and maiming second echelon soldiers. The longbow then was the first effective standoff weapon and a major improvement in weaponry.

Although Crécy marked the beginning of the end of chivalry on the battlefield, exposing the mounted knights' vulnerabilities to horse and body armor, it was the invention of gunpowder and its adoption to firearms and artillery that hastened the demise of feudalism, and dramatically changed the conduct of warfare. For centuries defense had generally dominated warfare. However, the advent of siege cannon changed all that. No longer were the defensive strongholds impregnable and little by little, they were dismantled. This led to the centralization of authority in regional entities and national states and to the formation of vastly larger armies.

The advent of firearms and artillery also had other major ramifications. Up until the fifteenth century, military hardware had been relatively inexpensive to make. Handheld weapons could be made easily by almost anyone. Now, economic factors became much more important. Not only were the weapons more costly but they were difficult to manufacture. Consequently, specialized munitions industries came into being. The increased range and destructive power of these new weapons revolutionized the organization and tactics of warfare and ushered in the period of "modern warfare." It was not until about 1450 that firearms and artillery had a role on the battlefield.

Gustavus Adolphus, (1594-1632) [3], focused on his Army's capabilities and he was responsible for the revamping of its organization, training, and equipment. He built the first truly national Army. Advances in metallurgy allowed him to cast smaller, four-pounder cannons that were light enough for several men or a horse to handle. This enabled the artillery to accompany the infantry into battles more readily. He reorganized the brigade as a tactical unit with separate companies and his cavalry was trained for reconnaissance and he organized a corps of sappers expert in bridging and constructing field fortifications. Through strict discipline he greatly reduced the size of his supply trains, increasing their march capability and enhancing mobility. He paid great attention to the soldiers' training, insisting upon coordination between units, so that for the first time, troops fought as combined arms...infantry, cavalry, and artillery. His tactical concept was two units forward and one unit in reserve to take advantage of tactical opportunities, a tactical formation in continuous use up to modern times. Gustavus Adolphus is often called the father of modern warfare.

When Frederick (1712-1786)[3], ascended to the throne of Prussia, a nation of only five million people in 1740, he immediately invaded Silesia, which was currently part of the Austrian Empire. His first military exploits enabled him to formulate a coherent military philosophy. Noting that his enemies were slow to react, he advanced the concept of mobility and the concentration of combat power. It seems that the emphasis of Gustavus Adolphus on mobility was lost on subsequent commanders whose movements were slow and mechanical. Frederick rigidly adhered to the principle of the offensive, and because he was almost always faced with superior numbers of troops, he realized that only by maneuver could he overcome this force ratio. To enhance mobility he built up his cavalry and developed horse artillery. He never neglected the training and equipping of his Army, always insisting upon the rigid discipline for which the Prussians were famous. Frederick brought great skill to the art of war, adhering to the principles of the offensive, mobility, and concentration of combat power. His emphasis on training and discipline was an important element in his Army's success.

On 23 August 1793, the new French Republic, issued a decree establishing universal conscription. France became the first nation-in-arms. Although the decree provided desperately-needed troops, it did not supply the military leadership, which was necessary to train the Army and lead it in battle. This leadership vacuum was eventually filled by Napoleon Bonaparte (1769-1821). Napoleon believed in rapid movement. His was an Army of infantrymen. They lived off the land with minimum supply trains. It was an axiom of Napoleon that the essence of strategy was to have more force than the enemy at the crucial point. He stated that the strength of an army was its momentum expressed as the mass multiplied by the velocity (basic Soviet doctrine).

The marriage of universal conscription with the capabilities of the nascent industrial revolution, greatly expanded the scope of war, increasing the number of combatants, the area, and the intensity.

With WORLD WAR I (1914-1918)[4] the growth of nationalism in Europe inflamed rivalries, particularly between France and Germany, as the major powers sought economic advantages. The major combatants, France, England, and Russia versus Germany and Austro-Hungary, each mobilized millions of men. It was a war on a scale never seen before.

The Germans attacked on 14 August, and for ten days there was a series of battles known as the Battle of the Frontiers, in which the Allies were decisively defeated and driven back, but they were able to regroup their

13

forces at the Marne River. The Allies were all but defeated but refused to give in and launched a counter-offensive on 6 September 1914. The Battle of the Marne was the decisive battle of World War I. The battle highlighted the importance of information (aerial reconnaissance showed the exposed German flank) and good communications (the lack of which caused the Germans to withdraw).

Subsequently, both sides dug in and prepared elaborate defensive positions. A virtual stalemate ensued. The machine gun took an enormous toll on lives. Firepower became ascendant over maneuver.

World War I saw the introduction of several important weapons and pieces of equipment, including the tank, airplane, motorized transport, and chemical weapons. But it was the scale of the conflict that was previously unfathomable, with over sixty million men mobilized and over eight million combatants killed or died from wounds. The rise of military industrial complexes initiated a spiral of increasing armament complexities.

In WORLD WAR II (1939-1945) the German Army, having conquered France and the Balkans, to secure its rear flank invaded Russia on 22 June 1941. Hitler's strategic plan, Case Barbarossa was bold. (see Map 1)

The strategic plan called for penetration by three Army Groups with the Central Army Group given the task of bursting forward with particularly strong Panzer and motorized formations from the area around and north of Warsaw and of smashing the enemy force in Byelorussia.

Although the German plan was simple in concept, it took tremendous logistical and operational planning if it were to be successful. By concentrating their forces, the Germans had a favorable force ratio of about five to one at the location of the main effort. On 22 June 1941, the two Panzer Armies penetrating across relatively narrow fronts burst forth with lightning speed. The high degree of mobility by the German infantry troops enabled them to closely support the armored forces and prevented the Russians from extricating themselves from the envelopments. The Panzer Armies successfully closed the Minsk pocket, capturing over 300,000 men and over 3,000 tanks. Continuing their rapid advance, the Central Army Group also enveloped Smolensk, capturing an additional 300,000 prisoners and 3,000 tanks. In this initial attack, the German losses were light, with 40,000 total casualties, killed and wounded[1].The efforts of the German Air Force prevented meaningful reinforcements. The spectacular support of the Luftwaffe was a major factor in the success of the ground forces.

Map 1

CASE BARBAROSSA

"GENERAL INTENTION: THE BULK OF THE RUSSIAN ARMY IN WESTERN RUSSION IS TO BE ANNIHILATD IN BOLD OPERATIONS BY DEEPLY PENETRATING PANZER WEDGES...HITLER. 18 DEC 1940"

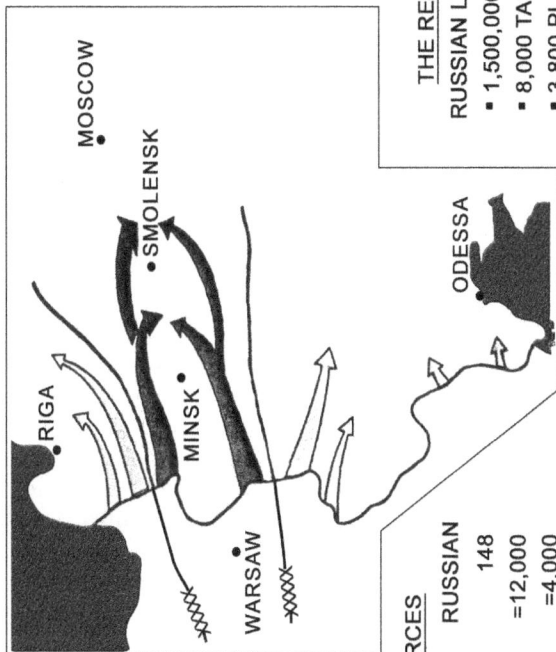

RIGA

MOSCOW

SMOLENSK

MINSK

WARSAW

ODESSA

THE RESULTS
RUSSIAN LOSSES
- 1,500,000 MEN
- 8,000 TANKS
- 3,800 PLANES

THE FORCES	GERMAN	RUSSIAN
DIV	135	148
TANKS	3,600	=12,000
PLANES	2,200	=4,000

Source: BDM, 1976

15

Case Barbarossa is cited as an excellent example of the utilization of modern equipment in a combined arms effort to effect maximum results. The success of the Germans was due to several factors: tactical surprise, concentration of force, the shock effect of armor, and the attainment of air superiority.

Operations had intensified in time and space, and military organizations had adapted to the utilization of faster, more lethal, and serviceable weapons. Many new and highly lethal weapons were introduced during the war: highly mobile and armored tanks, jet aircraft, ballistic missiles, and anti-aircraft guns, bombers, flame throwers, land mines, and atomic bombs, to name a few.

In Vietnam, (1965-1973)[5], the war and its total environment were so foreign to classical Western experiences that it was difficult to grasp. There were no set piece battles and it was difficult to differentiate combatants from the indigenous population. Only when cornered or when the odds looked favorable , as at Tet, would the communist accept combat. The terrain, from the heavy forested jungle to the inundated rice paddies of the Delta, mitigated against the use of heavy armored vehicles. Vietnam was a "grunts" war. The infantryman was the cutting edge of combat and as such he was also the most vulnerable. In this guerilla environment, with the enemy avoiding combat, a premium was placed on intelligence efforts and, the unconventional warfare called for new strategies. The conflict was to gain control of land and population. It took time for the South Vietnamese government to expand its regional forces (RF/PF) and to establish a two million village defense force (PSDF) that could maintain control over those areas secured by Allied regular troops, thus permitting pacification and economic development to occur.

On 6 October 1973, the Jewish high holy day of Yom Kippur, both Syria and Egypt initiated limited objective surprise attacks on Israel, the Syrians against the Golan Heights and the Egyptians crossing the Suez and attacking into the Sinai. The Israeli military, relying primarily upon its mobile armored formations and air force for orchestrating firepower, immediately counterattacked. The Arabs responded with anti-tank guided missiles (ATGMs) and the Israeli armored force lost three-fourths of its approximately 450 initially dispersed tanks in the first eighteen hours of battle[6]. Recognizing that their armor was vulnerable to ATGMs, the Israelis immediately changed tactics by having infantry troops accompany their armored units. This combined arms tactic greatly reduced further tank losses, and verified the importance of combined arms operations. Again, both in the ground and in the air, the superior aptitude and training of the

Israelis had a significant impact, enabling them to overcome the much larger Arab forces.

Subsequently military planners wondered whether the critical role of the tank in combat had been severely denigrated by ATGMs. Others were concerned with the effectiveness of surface-to-air missiles against close support aircraft. The relationship of weapon lethality versus survivability often dictated tactics, and over the centuries the trends of warfare have varied between the offense and the defensive, the "yin and yang" of combat. In the modern period, the spirit of the offensive has dominated. In 1975 the tank, however, remained the decisive tactical weapon in the central duel of combat.

In this cursory review of the changing character of warfare, it can be seen that the numbers, mechanization, mobility and lethality of equipment continuously grew throughout the ages, as did the size of armies, the frequency of battles, and the range of operations. The tempo and intensity of warfare has grown almost exponentially. Consequently, today's soldiers must be better trained than ever in order to operate the complex equipment and to function well on the currently stressful battlefield. Strategy has not changed much and the Principles of War have remained inviolate. Basic tactics in general have changed little.

It is the intensity and speed of combat that requires lower echelon commanders to grasp possible alternatives and to act quickly and decisively that is vitally different. Today, the techniques of commanders in utilizing their resources often spells victory or defeat.

It is the equipment and weapons of war that have changed dramatically, as have their costs. The question facing decision-makers in 1975 was how to integrate the myriad of current weaponry and to develop new ones so as to insure the most effective force structure. Tactics and training are for the most part a function of the force structure, which was also evolving as the result of the development of new combat systems.

One could say prior to World War II that combat could be described as the "Age of Infantry." However, Germany's "Blitzkrieg" tactics in World War II ushered in the "Age of Armor," and it will remain so until really effective anti-armor weapons are developed. Many thought after the short Yom Kippur War that the ATGMs had sounded the death knell to armor, but it will be shown that this was not the case.

Today, there is much better detection of the enemy. The many tactical sensors available today can detect most enemy activities. The Army could also accomplish that in the Vietnam Conflict and in Desert Storm, however, often the information was not transmitted to the action point in time to be acted upon. Battlefield information and effective command and control are the keys to victory.

This book has been written to explain the pertinent steps taken by BSI in the mid-seventies to determine the most effective battlefield systems architecture for the Army which was constantly improving its combat systems, doctrine, training and techniques. It is hoped that the type of analyses taken then might be of value today in developing the army's transformation, particularly the input-output cost analysis and the method of relating technology to battlefield systems. The integrative efforts of the mid 1970s paid off in the battles of the Iraq War. The transformational efforts of today may well be tested twenty years from now.

A major requirement existed in 1975 to integrate the expanding inventory of equipment so as to have the maximum effectiveness on the battlefield at the most reasonable cost. How this overriding requirement for *Battlefield Systems Integration* was accomplished is the subject of this book.

REQUIREMENTS FOR
BATTLEFIELD SYSTEMS INTEGRATION

For a decade, the wars in Southeast Asia (SEA) had absorbed the concentration of the US military establishment. The substantial funding increases of the period had resulted in the development of greatly improved conventional tactical weapons systems such as helicopters, precision guided missiles, improved munitions, target acquisition systems, night vision devices, navigation and positioning systems, anti-aircraft systems, and radar tracking systems. However, the perception that these weapon systems had not been tied together into an effective overall operating system was being keenly felt by personnel in the Department of the Army. Additionally, the concentration on the SEA battlefields had allowed the Soviets to surpass the US in several important areas of technology and military capabilities. Trends at this time were clearly in the Soviet's favor. Concurrently with the termination of hostilities in SEA, the military budgets were being severely reduced. Thus, there was an overriding requirement to develop and deploy weapons systems that were both performance and cost effective.

In early 1974, the Wakelin Committee, composed of distinguished scientists, produced a report which stated[1]:

> "...the ability to see the combat fighting effectiveness of the Army in the context of an integrated, carefully balanced system is so fractionated within the Army as to bring into serious question whether or not the Army in the field has been adequately considered as an integrated system."

Later, on 31 December 1974, in a letter to the Secretary of the Army, Mr. Charles L. Poor, the Deputy Assistant Secretary of the Army (Research and Development) stated[2]:

> "I believe we are confined by a deeply rooted organizational defect that has limited our effectiveness in development planning in the past, and will continue to do so in the future, if not remedied soon. The absence of an Integrated System Design Agency with a balanced staff chartered to consider the Army as a system is the organizational defect."

Thus it was recognized by senior personnel that the Army's current method of developing advanced concepts of systems and doctrines within the compartmented structure of the many functionally oriented development centers, the so-called commodity commands, and the various branch service schools had the defect of not adequately addressing interfaces and the total workings of the system.

Subsequently, on 1 May, the Secretary of the Army, Mr. Bo Callaway, stated in a memorandum[3]: "Several people have concurred in the need to have a capability to look at our weapons systems in the context of a total system. This should enable us to exploit the small advantages of a single system by seeking its interaction with all other systems on the battlefield. We need to push this idea into the creation of a small, talented, imaginative operating organization."

The responsibility for implementing the Secretary of the Army's decision was given to General Jack Deane, the newly assigned CG of the Army Materiel Command. Subsequently, in August 1975, I was assigned as the Director of the Office of Battlefield Systems Integration (BSI), given a blank sheet of paper, and told to organize the office. To insure coordination between the developers and the users, the Director of Battlefield Systems Integration was to report to both the CGs of the Materiel Command and the Training and Doctrine Command.

To create an organizational structure it was a priori essential to define the mission of BSI. The BSI Mission was defined by the Department of the Army to: treat Army in the field as a total system, integrated with other services to maximize total system capabilities; identify gaps in current and future battle systems; submit recommendations to realize the full potential of technology; participate in current combat development/materiel acquisition activities; apply in-house and contractual analyses to optimize combat systems development; assure that materiel development programs are consistent with evolving TRADOC doctrinal concepts; sponsor prototype demonstrations of combat systems.

A review of the mission statement indicates that the BSI was faced with a herculean task and one that would depend primarily upon a proper organization manned with outstanding personnel. The function of systems integration was inherently difficult for the Army to address. The acquisition system was asked to implement requirements that had been largely defined by user agencies, often with rigorous time and cost limits. Reconciliation of demands of the "User" and the "Developer" and coordination of programs within the budget and fiscal process was a fundamental problem. Since

Army systems are not usually functionally independent and complete, they must perform in a complex operational environment in conjunction with other systems. Unquestionably, the challenge for the development and acquisition of equipment centered upon questions of systems interfaces and systems integration.

The requirement for the interaction of systems suggested an organization along broad functional or mission-oriented lines. Also, to insure the close coordination between user and developer, it was deemed essential to have a close tie-in with TRADOC service schools, where system requirements originated with the concomitant requirements for manpower and training which were so important in life cycle cost considerations. With the increased pressure of reduced funding for the acquisition of Army weapon systems, the cost aspect was vital. Consequently, we molded the two ideas of service school coordination and OSD budgetary program mission areas in considering the BSI organization.

We also had to consider a broad functional structure along technical lines. Although a technical approach did not lend itself to the assignment of responsibilities for specific integration problems, it was essential that a technical capability exist.

After much consideration, it was decided to develop a matrix type organization. Although the size of BSI had been recommended to be between 75 and 100 personnel, I opted for a much smaller office for several reasons. Most importantly I wanted all assigned personnel to be able to interact closely and continually. There would be no layering. Another consideration for designing a smaller office was the staffing problem. Finding personnel within the Army with the requisite skills and, more importantly, the experience covering the full range of technical, operational and management problems, would be difficult. Once personnel were identified, being able to pry such valuable people out of the personnel system would be very difficult and time-consuming at best. To be effective, BSI required immediate staffing.

Understandably, a small, dynamic, highly qualified staff could not possibly perform the complex missions assigned, so outside contractual assistance would be required. It was hoped to be able to contract for a not-for-profit research organization, particularly one which had been designated as a Federal Contract Research Center (FCRC). Importantly, a FCRC would have no hardware equipment development or profit motivations. Because of the perceived importance of BSI, the OSD Director of Research and Engineering on 30 October authorized the Army to increase its MITRE effort for the Battlefield Systems Integration Program to an annual level of 32 ½ MTS within the current Army FCRC ceiling. This approval required the Army to redistribute previously allocated FCRC work[4]. Consequently, on 15 January 1976, the Army revised its program within ceiling constraints, reducing the allocation of the Lincoln Laboratory and the Applied Physics Laboratory to accommodate an increase in the funding level of MITRE. I was extremely pleased to obtain such a prestigious organization as MITRE to support our efforts. Additionally, BSI also had line-item funding authorized which enabled it to contract with highly qualified civilian research organizations.

The grade structure of the military personnel was approved by DCSPER on 19 September 1975. However, to obtain the essential technically qualified civilian personnel it was necessary to establish four civilian super grade positions, and these positions were subject to approval by the US Civil Service Commission. The approved organization is shown on Chart 1. Thus, by February 1976, BSI had almost all its personnel and its contracting capabilities and was ready to roll.

Chart 1

ORGANIZATIONAL CHART
DIRECTORATE FOR BATTLEFIELD SYSTEMS INTEGRATION

Director	MG
Deputy Director	PL 313
Associate Director for	
Physical Science	PL 313
Executive Officer	05
Secretary	GS-09
Secretary	GS-08

SYSTEMS DIRECTORS

Infantry	06
Armor	06
Artillery	06
Aviation	06
Combat Spt - Nuclear	06
Military Intelligence	06
Command, Control, Communications	06
Air Defense	06
Logistics	06
Clerk/Steno	GS-05

TECHNICAL OFFICE

Assistant for Aero Eng	GS-16*
Assistant for Electronics	GS-16*
Operations Research Analyst	GS-15
Systems Engineer	GS-15
Operations Research Analyst	GS-15
(COST)	
Clerk/Steno	GS-05

*Subject to approval by US Civil Service Commission.

Source: Office of Battlefield Systems Integration, 1975

23

BATTLEFIELD SYSTEMS ARCHITECTURE

Conceptually, it was believed in higher headquarters that technological advances in battlefield surveillance, communications, and the guidance of armaments when effectively integrated could lead to major increases in overall war fighting capabilities...the force multiplier effect. The Army's in-house development centers, working closely with industry, are continually developing new and more lethal and serviceable weapons systems, creating the necessity to consider which of these potential systems should be integrated into the force structure and what would their impact be upon the operational aspects of training, doctrine, and tactics. Attempting to forecast technological advances leading to potentially new systems which are required to be integrated while at the same time determining optimum numbers and types of systems within given cost parameters which should exist on the battlefield is a much less defined and difficult undertaking...that of determining a battlefield architecture.

Architecture, then, is an <u>evolutionary</u> plan <u>synchronizing</u> the development of doctrine, forces, materiel, and technology. The determination of a battlefield systems architecture was the task of BSI. The methodology which BSI adopted to develop an architecture will be discussed later. Realistically, the payoffs of an effective architecture could be huge, some of which are to:

- Ensure interoperability of Army capabilities.
- Identify gaps and deficiencies in Army capabilities.
- Link mission context with technical innovations.
- Identify near term product improvements.
- Identify significant issues and alternatives.
- Improve cost/benefit ratios
- Integrate other service and national assets.

The bottom line was that the US Army must be fully trained and prepared to fight fast-paced, combined arms battles with reliable, highly lethal equipment and WIN!

The equipment challenge was: What do we need? and What can we afford?.

This was to be accomplished by determining a battlefield architecture by close coordination with the user, utilizing the full potential of technology, grasping materiel opportunities, and systems planning and design; to insure creative system design, and integrate current systems; thereby synergizing Army capabilities.

HOW THE ARMY FIGHTS

One Fall day in 1975, at TRADOC Headquarters, General DePuy, the TRADOC Commander, and I were doing a blackboard analysis in his office on the conduct of battle – How the Army Fights. We started out, obviously, discussing the main battle area, the CLOSE COMBAT. However, prior to the initial engagement, our Intelligence/Surveillance/Target Acquisition (ISTA) systems were attempting to locate the enemy and divine his intentions. When targeted, our FIRE SUPPORT artillery, mortars, rockets and missiles were called up to fire upon the enemy's first and second echelon troops, and once the enemy had closed, to support our combat troops in contact. Concurrently, our AIR DEFENSE units were engaging the enemy tactical air. OTHER COMBAT SUPPORT units, such as engineers, were creating obstacles and mine fields to channel the attacking force into our killing zones while the COMBAT SERVICE SUPPORT troops were busy replacing ammunition, maintaining equipment, and providing medical evacuation and treatment. Further to the rear the LOGISTIC units were busy stockpiling supports and equipment. All of the foregoing activities were constantly being monitored and information was being transmitted by COMMAND SYSTEMS.

Shortly thereafter I noted that the office of the Secretary of Defense had established Standard Capability Categories in order to segregate and analyze the myriad of Army systems for their programming and budgetary reviews. The over 500 major Army systems had been divided into thirty-nine functional groups of systems and each functional group had been assigned to one of the above mentioned nine mission areas.

Close Combat
Fire Support
Other Combat Support
Air Defense
Intelligence, Surveillance, and Target Acquisition
Command Systems
Command Services Support
Other Logistics
Other

In reality, these capability categories summarized our previous blackboard analysis of "How the Army Fights." A matrix of the mission areas and the functional group of systems would be an outstanding method of

Chart 2

THE STRUCTURE OF OPERATIONAL FUCNTIONS

MISSION AREAS \ FUNCTIONAL GROUPS OF SYSTEMS	TANK	MECH INF	ANTI-TANK	COMBAT AVIATION	LIGHT WEAPONS	MORTARS	CANNON ARTILLERY	ROCKETS/MISSILES	NIGHT OBSERVATIONS	COMBAT ENGINEER	MINE/COUNTERMINE	NBC	COMBAT SPT SUPPORT	SHORT RANGE AD SYSTEMS	MEDIUM RANGE AD SYSTEMS	LONG RANGE AD SYSTEMS	AIR DEFENSE SUPPORT	RECON/SURV/TGT ACQ	SIGINT	EW	STRATEGIC INTEL	INTEL SUPPORT	POSITION LOCATION	STRATEGIC COMMO	TACTICAL CAMMO	COMSEC	AUTOMATION	OTHER C₃	SUPPLY & TRANSPORTATION	MAINTENANCE	MEDICAL	ENERGY	AVIATION SUPPORT	OTHER COMBAT SVC SUPPORT	FIXED WING AIRCRAFT	ADMIN VEHICLES	CONSTRUCTION	OTHER LOGISTICS	TRAINING DEVICES	TOTAL
CLOSE COMBAT	X	X	X	X	X																																			
FIRE SUPPORT						X	X	X																																
OTHER COMBAT SPT									X	X	X	X	X																											
AIR DEFENSE														X	X	X	X																							
INTEL/SURV/TGT ACQ																		X	X	X	X	X																		
COMMAND SYSTEMS																							X	X	X	X	X	X												
COMBAT SERVICE SPT																													X	X	X	X	X	X						
OTHER LOGISTICS																																			X	X	X	X		
OTHER																																							X	
TOTAL																																								

Source: Office of Battlefield Systems Integration, 1976

27

categorizing and reviewing Army systems requirements and developments. It would mesh with current programming reviews and it would insure that no major system would be neglected in analyses.

The matrix, which was approved by the Department of the Army[1], provided the basis for analysis to determine the two key factors of <u>costs</u> and <u>combat effectiveness.</u> As previously stated, within the nine mission areas there were thirty-nine functional groups of systems and within these thirty-nine groups there were over 500 systems. Not all systems were by any means vital, but all contributed to the Army's combat power and all had to be reviewed to examine interoperability, identify gaps and eliminate duplication.

To obtain a complete portrayal of "How the Army Fights," we also had to include the vital role of the US Tactical Air Force which attacked the enemy in the main battle area as well as deep into enemy territory to disrupt his ability to move and to mass his forces. Additionally, the Air Force and the National Systems were important players in providing inputs into the ISTA mission area by collecting information from aerial and satellite surveillance and communications intercepts. The total portrayal of "How the Army Fights" is depicted in Chart 3.

To achieve our goals of producing system concepts and fostering developments which treated the Army in the field as a total cohesive system, integrated so that combat subsystems, including appropriate components of the US Air Force, are configured to operate in a common architecture which would maximize the total system capabilities, BSI would have to formulate specific objectives and plans for each of the broad mission areas, taking into account current operational capabilities, technology forecasts and threat assessments.

Chart 3

HOW THE ARMY FIGHTS

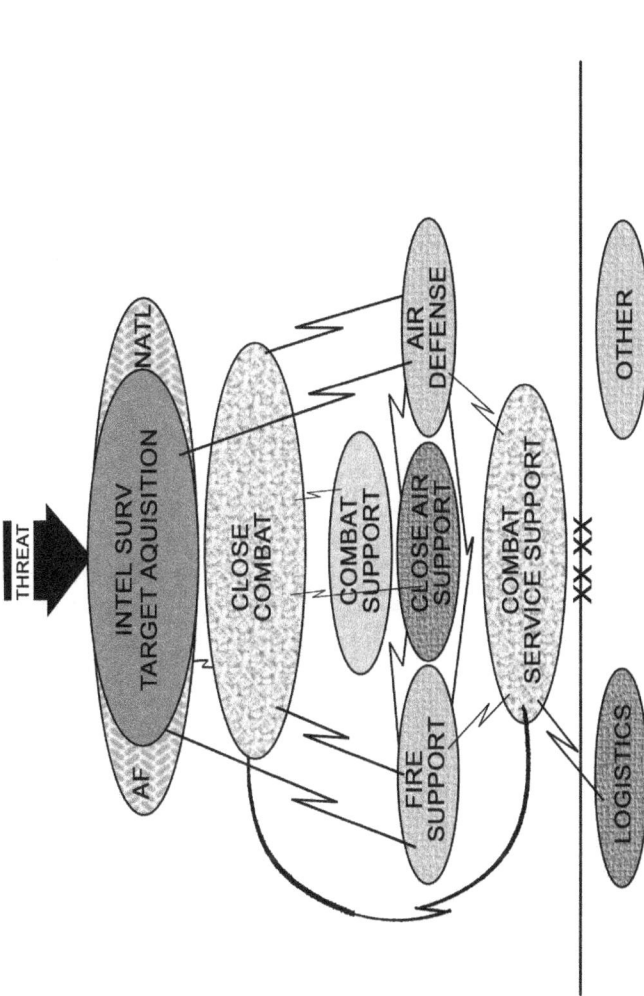

THREAT

INTEL SURV
TARGET AQUISITION

NATL

AF

CLOSE
COMBAT

COMBAT
SUPPORT

CLOSE AIR
SUPPORT

AIR
DEFENSE

FIRE
SUPPORT

COMBAT
SERVICE SUPPORT

XX XX

LOGISTICS

OTHER

Source: Office of Battlefield Systems Integration/MITRE, 1977

29

RELATING TECHNOLOGY PROGRAMS TO BATTLEFIELD SYSTEMS

In order to participate in current combat development and materiel acquisition activities, and apply in-house and contractual analyses to optimize combat system developments while assuring that materiel development programs were consistent with evolving TRADOC doctrinal concepts it was necessary to be able to catalogue the current DARCOM Base Technology Programs and relate them to battlefield systems. Cataloging the technology base was in itself a daunting task, yet it was only a partial requirement.

The Army's technology programs must be objective oriented, that is, attempting to solve the user's priority requirements for systems improvements and upgrading capabilities. The Department of the Army annually publishes the Science and Technology Guide (STOG), a requirements document which translates mission deficiencies and capability gaps into broad science and technology objectives. Therefore the technology base had to be related to both the STOs and to the mission areas and functional groups of systems previously discussed and the user/developer proponent relationship had to be identified. Ultimately, it was imperative to correlate development costs with battlefield effectiveness.

I had heard that the Army Materials and Mechanics Research Center in Watertown, Massachusetts had developed a methodology that could possibly be utilized to catalogue the Army Science and Technology base providing a quick look at battlefield systems. Therefore, I visited Dr. John Burke and his team at Watertown to review his "SPIDER Chart" methodology. It was tailor made for BSI requirements, enabling the technology base to be related to standard capability categories (mission areas/functional groups) and providing a capability to analyze and revise the Army's prioritized objectives (STOs). SPIDER is an acronym for Systematic Planning for the Integration of Defense Engineering and Research. We selected the method because its graphic display provides a logical and sequential relationship between the current operational and future needs of battlefield systems and the work being done in the DARCOM laboratories and by industry. It also provided a mechanism for TRADOC to promote user inputs into the base technology programs.

The charting system we developed depicts the flow of information essential to make useful evaluations (Chart 4). Within the users (ie: TRADOC schools) area of responsibility for developing concepts and establishing requirements, the information flow included the mission area, the functional group of systems, systems, sub-subsystems, STOG priorities and operational capability requirements. Within the developers (ie: the DARCOM commodity commands) area of responsibility for developing technology and making technical decisions, the flow continued to include the pacing problems preventing achievement of the operational capability requirement and the work unit necessary to solve the problem as well as the responsible DARCOM Commodity Command and the TRADOC School proponency to include it's priority of the work.

With respect to the operational capabilities which enabled the mission to be achieved, we recommended a standard set of six battlefield capabilities to describe any system: firepower, mobility, survivability/vulnerability, communications, sensing, and support. Some complex systems might have all six capabilities while other specialized systems might have only one or two capabilities that describe their function. Each capability has a standard set of between six and fourteen subsystems associated with it.

The operational capability requirement is a statement of the users technology base requirement at the subsystem level and is a subset of a specific Science and Technology Objective (STO) which for the most part describes a system or a capability. The pacing problem is a statement of the technical barrier that must be overcome to achieve the operational capability requirement.

To further illustrate the charting system let us consider the VIPER, the light anti-tank missile system under development, which is one of the twelve systems in the anti-tank group of systems within the close combat mission area. In 1975 one of the DOD strategic objectives was that NATO forces must be able to defend against a potential Soviet attack in Central Europe. Any conflict in Europe with all its built-up areas would see continuous fighting in cities and towns. The Israeli experience in Beirut indicated that we definitely needed to acquire much more knowledge in this type of warfare. The fighting in Beirut was at very close quarters and, as an example, the light anti-tank weapon (LAW) would not arm because the length of flight of the missile to the target was less than the required arming distance of the weapon. Also there was a lack of data concerning the effect of the LAW against structures in order to dislodge enemy combatants. Therefore, for the VIPER system there was an operational capability

Chart 4

RELATING TECHNOLOGY PROGRAMS to BATTLEFIELD SYSTEMS

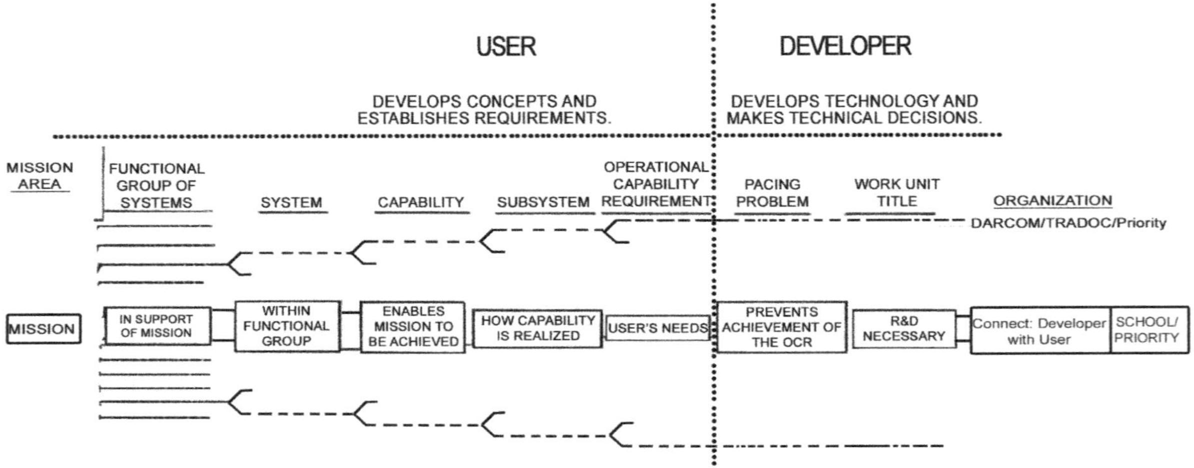

Source: Office of Battlefield Systems Integration/Army Materials and Mechanics Research Center (AMMRC), 1976

requirement to effectively operate in built up areas and two of its pacing problems were to reduce the arming distance and to obtain data concerning the weapons capabilities against structures.

Chart 5 depicts the VIPER's firepower capability which has six potential subsystems and in this case the launcher subsystem has been considered and the operational capability requirement was operations in built-up areas. The pacing problem was a lack of combat data and the work unit was an analysis of composite building structures. Also listed is the DARCOM Missile Laboratory as the responsible developer and the TRADOC Infantry School as the user proponent with a C (low) priority.

SPIDER charts were helpful in the management and control of the Army R&D efforts. The graphical logic of the SPIDER charts primarily permitted the clear identification of gaps and redundancies with regard to priorities established by the user and they brought together for the first time a comprehensive listing of R&D work units in their operational context. Allocation of R&D efforts should be made on the basis of the potential contributions to combat effectiveness as well as by scientific opportunity. We often found that the user was not onboard with many of the developer's efforts.

When the SPIDER charts for the total Army technology base were completed there were:

183	Science and Technology Objectives
738	Operational Capability Requirements
1943	Pacing Problems

BSI's interests were concerned with improving the user-developer dialogue as well as insuring battlefield effectiveness. Obviously not all the operational capability requirements would provide major improvements in combat effectiveness, particularly when reviewed by the responsible service schools and integrated by TRADOC[1]. Hq TRADOC was requested to review each work unit to verify the proponent school and to establish a priority for the work unit corresponding to the following code:

A	Critical
B	Essential
C	Required
D	No specific Interest.

Chart 5

THE VIPER LAUNCHER SUB-SYSTEM

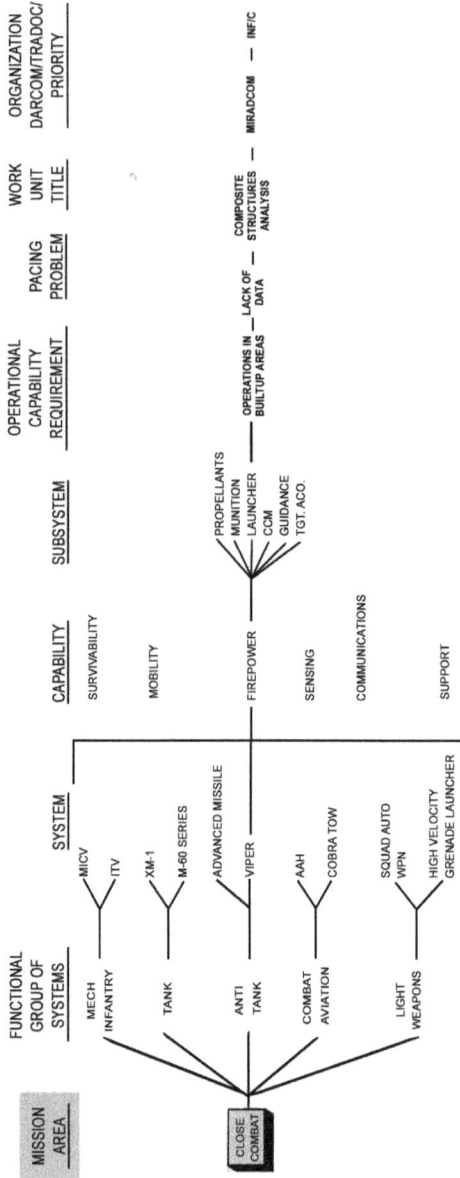

Source: Office of Battlefield Systems Integration/Army Materials and Mechanics Research Center (AMMRC), 1976

The analysis of the priorities assigned by proponent users to existing work units is shown in Chart 6. The results of this evaluation are most interesting, for among the 2040 work units reported only 12 were rated as critical and 181 were rated essential. Two-thirds of the work units received a C priority, and nearly one-fourth were rated "No Specific Interest." The Infantry School considered only 39 out of 544 (7.1%) close combat work units to be critical or essential. Obviously, there was a **major disconnect** between the user and the developer. Many users who had recently completed field duty were often concerned with current problems faced by tactical units whereas developers were generally more focused on new technology. Also, it should be noted that the work units which were more technical in nature or had a distant payoff tended to have lower assigned priorities.

In several cases the developer had major funded work units in areas that were low on the user's priority list and vice versa. We also found user proponent schools often were not familiar with the pacing problems of essential operational capability requirements. In other words, there had been a lack of coordination between the user and developer. It appeared sometimes that the developer was engaged in "pet" projects to the detriment of solving user requirements. At the time perhaps the least effective mission area overall was the all-important command systems. Yet, command systems had zero critical priority work units and only 3% of its work units were considered essential. There was not sufficient focus on this critical mission area. Closer coordination between the user and developer was necessary to identify R&D efforts with their potential contributions to combat effectiveness and structured programs were necessary to provide for the most effective allocation of resources and the comparative evaluation of concepts.

The SPIDER charts for the first time enabled users and developers to focus on technology expenditures in mission areas broken down into the capabilities of systems thereby enabling systems development to mesh with the established user priorities.

The allocation of technology based FY 77 funding is shown in Chart 7 by mission areas and functional groups of systems. In the $73 million allocated to close combat only $2 million, or 2.7%, was provided for research in the important anti-tank functional group. This glaring deficiency was rectified in FY 78 when 21% of the close combat funding was allocated to anti-tank.

Chart 6
USER PROPONENT PRIORITIES
BY NUMBER OF WORK UNITS
AND ARMY MISSION AREA

Priority Ratings

Mission Area	A	B	C	D		Totals
Close Combat	6 (1%)	33 (6%)	308 (57%)	197 (36%)		544
Other Combat Support		26 (9%)	214 (73%)	54 (18%)	*	294
Combat Service Support		20 (6%)	229 (65%)	101 (29%)		350
Fire Support	1 (.5%)	27 (12%)	121 (56%)	68 (31%)		217
Air Defense	2 (1%)	32 (20%)	108 (70%)	12 (8%)		154
ISTA	3 (2%)	36 (20%)	114 (63%)	29 ((16%)		182
Command Systems		7 (3%)	174 (90%)	13 (6%)		194
Program-Wide Support			51 (100%			51
Other Logistics			19 (80%)	5 (20%)		24
Ballistic Missile Defense			30 (100%)			30
Totals	12 (.6%)	181 (9%)	1368 (67%)	479 (23%)		2040

Source: Office of Battlefield Systems Integration/Army Materials and Mechanics Research Center (AMMRC) and TRADOC Schools, 1976

The percent of funding for close combat capabilities is indicated by the following table.

Table 1
R&D Funding for Close Combat Capabilities

Capability	Funding
Firepower	29.5
Mobility	18.9
Survivability/Vulnerability	17.4
Sensing	15.0
Communications	11.7
Support	7.5

The critical sensing capabilities had only 15% of close combat funding and even less (11%) in the FY 78 program. Funding for these critical capabilities must be improved.

In attempting to determine which of the potentially new combat systems to consider to integrate into the force structure and particularly what would be the system impact on operations, training, doctrine and tactics it is essential not only that the Army's in-house developmental centers and industry work closely together but that the user is continuously on board during the developmental process, particularly in determining priorities. SPIDER charts enabled user proponent schools and developer laboratories to focus on the pacing problems of operational capabilities by systems within functional groups thus enabling gaps and under-funded areas to be identified.

Chart 7
RESEARCH FUNDING
BY MISSION AREA and OPERATIONAL FUNCTION
FY 1977 (DOLLARS IN MILLIONS)

MISSION AREAS	FUNCTIONAL GROUPS OF SYSTEMS	PROGRAM CATEGORY			MISSION AREA TOTAL	MISSION AREA PERCENT
		6.2	6.3A	TOTAL		
CLOSE COMBAT	TANK	14.4	2.7	17.1		
	MEC_TANK	6.8	4.7	11.5		
	ANTI-TANK	--	2	2.0		
	COMBAT AVIATION	24.7	12.3	37.0		
	LIGHT WEAPONS	2.4	3	5.4	73.0	12.8%
FIRE SUPPORT	MORTARS	5.6	--	5.6		
	CANNON ARTILLERY	13.8	4.7	18.5		
	ROCKETS/MISSILES	53.0	3.8	56.8		
	FIRE SPT SUPPORT	0.8	--	0.8	81.7	14.3
OTHER COMBAT SUPPORT	NIGHT OBSERVATIONS	9.9	--	9.9		
	COMBAT ENGINEER	4.5	0.8	5.3		
	MINE/COUTUREMINE	5.0	6.1	11.1		
	NBC	40.2	0.4	40.6		
	COMBAT SPT SUPPORT	5.7	1.3	7.0	73.9	12.9
AIR DEFENSE	SHORT RANGE AD SYSTEMS	--	28.3	28.3		
	MEDIUM RANGE AD SYSTEMS	--	--	--		
	LONG RANGE AD SYSTEMS	--	--	--		
	AIR DEFENSE SUPPORT	--	17.5	17.5	45.8	8.0
COMBAT SERVICE SUPPORT	SUPPLY & TRANSPORTATION	0.3	1.9	2.2		
	MAINTENANCE	--	0.8	0.8		
	MEDICAL	30.4	0.1	30.5		
	ENERGY	3.5	4.4	7.9		
	AVIATION SUPPORT	--	12.9	12.9		
	OTHER COMBAT SVC SUPPORT	1.0	--	1.0	55.3	9.7
INTEL/ SURV/ TGT ACQ	RECON/SURV./TGT ACQ.	22.5	4.4	26.9		
	SIGINT	--	--	--		
	EW	2.8	17.9	20.7		
	STRATEGIC INTEL.	--	--	--		
	INTEL. SUPPORT	3.1	0.4	3.5	51.1	9.0
COMMAND SYSTEMS	POSITION LOCATION	0.7	--	0.7		
	STRATEGIC COMMO	--	--	--		
	TACTICAL COMMO	5.4	--	5.4		
	COMSEC	--	--	--		
	AUTOMATION	4.4	6.6	11.0		
	OTHER C.	0.9	--	0.9	18	3.2
OTHER LOGISTICS	FIXED WING AIRCRAFT	--	--	--		
	ADMIN VEHICLES	--	--	--		
	CONSTRUCTION	7.6	0.8	8.4		
	OTHER LOGISTICS	10.3	0.9	11.2	19.6	3.4
OTHER	TRAINING DEVICES	5.9	3.8	9.7		
	MANPOWER	10.8	9.5	20.3		
	BDM	--	106.8	106.8	136.8	26.7
NOT COMBAT RELATED	NOT COMBAT RELATED	13.2	3.1	16.3	16.3	
	TOTAL	309.6	261.9	571.5	571.5	100%

Source: Army Material Command, 1976

INPUT-OUTPUT COST ANALYSIS

The SPIDER charts were significant to the Army's R&D management efforts because they represented an attempt to link operational requirements with technological development. The approved funding (costs) were a clear yardstick of program emphasis. But this of itself was not sufficient to depict the total picture. What was needed was a method to determine the basic life cycle costs of actually fielded major units (corps and divisions) to assess the interconnection of investment, military personnel (MPA) and operations and maintenance (OMA). The man-machine interface is of vital importance in determining the twin trade-offs of costs and combat effectiveness. However, it was more important to determine the answer to the question, "Where is our money going?"

Previously I had used Input-Output (1-O) analysis to show that funds committed to the Department of Defense would create more jobs in America than the same amount of funds provided to any other economic sector, such as construction or manufacturing[1]. As a consequence, I thought that I-O methods could be utilized to develop a specialized cost analysis technique to assist BSI in the performance of its responsibilities. I-O analysis is based upon the interdependencies between various sectors. The method is commonly used for estimating the impacts of positive or negative occurrences and analyzing the ripple effects. In our study of the total costs of a notional corps, the model quantifies in matrix form (see Chart 11) the interdependencies between the Army's thirty-nine functional groups of systems (horizontal) and the Army's standardized appropriation categories (vertical).

For some time the Army has had techniques and systems for the analysis of total Army force structures and individual weapon and support systems. What it did not have in 1976 was a technique which focused specifically on major combat forces in the battlefield and which enabled analysis of costs not only by standard appropriation categories, but also by the military missions or functions for which expenditures are incurred.

Mr. Robert Verbeck of BSI, ably supported by the computational capabilities and staff of MITRE, undertook the development of a closed system cost analysis technique which was a highly complex and laborious process. It was a unique model for the use of input-output analysis to analyze military life-cycle costs[2].

The objective was to be able to assess the structure and distribution of the life-cycle costs of acquisition and operation of major battlefield forces for periods of ten, twenty, or more years. Better understanding of important cost relationships were obtained: high cost areas were identified; areas which were more labor intensive were distinguished from those which were less labor intensive; and secondary and tertiary costs associated with primary military activities were identified.

Every operational division and corps in the Army is unique. Accordingly, for the purpose of developing this analytical technique, BSI elected to use notional force units rather than actual units. The US Army Command and General Staff College defined the composition of the notional corps for BSI and furnished a troop list for this study. The notional corps consisted of two armored divisions, one mechanized infantry division, one armored cavalry regiment, and one separate mechanized brigade, together with appropriate combat support and combat service support units. A list of units in this notional corps is provided in Table 2. Organizational diagrams of the notional armored division appear as Chart 8. The notional mechanized infantry division is quite similar to the notional armored division, except that it has six mechanized infantry battalions (whereas the armored division has five) and only four tank battalions (whereas the armored division has six). The matrix of standard capability categories for materiel acquisition (Chart 2) as well as the standard appropriation categories shown in Table 3 were utilized.

Table 2
Composition of Notional Corps

Armored Division	(2)	Combat Aviation Battalion	(1)
Mechanized Infantry Division	(1)	Combat Engineer Brigade	(1)
Armored Cavalry Regiment	(1)	ASA Battalion	(1)
Separate Mechanized Infantry Bde	(1)	CBTI Group	(1)
Field Artillery Group	(2)	Signal Group	(1)
Air Defense Artillery Group	(1)	COSCOM	(1)
Attack Helicopter Battalion	(1)	HHC, Corps	(1)

Chart 8

NOTIONAL ARMORED DIVISION ORGANIZATIONAL CHART

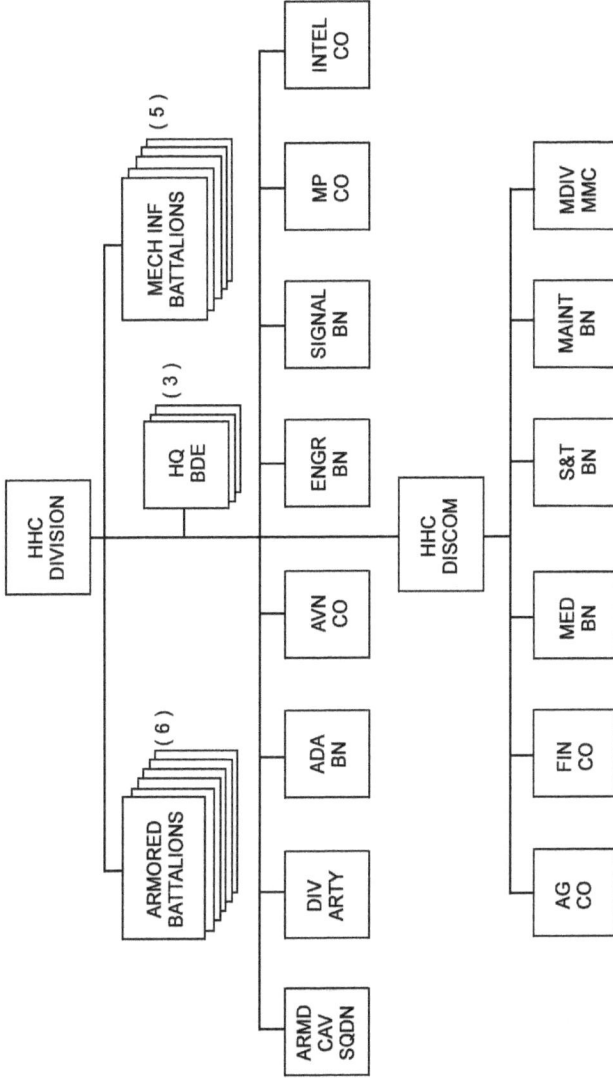

HHC DIVISION

ARMORED BATTALIONS (6)

HQ BDE (3)

MECH INF BATTALIONS (5)

ARMD CAV SQDN

DIV ARTY

ADA BN

AVN CO

ENGR BN

SIGNAL BN

MP CO

INTEL CO

HHC DISCOM

AG CO

FIN CO

MED BN

S&T BN

MAINT BN

MDIV MMC

Source: Army Command and General Staff College, 1977

41

Table 3
Coverage of Appropriation Categories

INVESTMENT
Procurement of Major Equipment
Operational Readiness Float
Repair Cycle Float
Repair Parts & Secondary Items
Ammunition Reserve
Wartime Active Replacement Reserve
MILITARY PERSONNEL
Pay & Allowances
Accession
Training
Permanent Change of Station
OPERATIONS & MAINTENANCE
OMA Prescribed Load List Repair Parts
Minor Equipment
Organization Clothing & Equipment
Unit Operating Costs
Base Operations (OMA P2)
Central Supply Activities (OMA P7 (S))
Depot Maintenance (OMA P8 (M))
Base Medical Cost (OMA P8 (M))
Training (OMA P8 (T))
Accession Processing and Support (OMA P8 (O))
Administrative and Other (OMA P9)

Standard Army sources were used to obtain all data in the development of this analysis technique, so that the results would be valid and compatible with other Army planning data. Use of such data was also desired so that the technique could be easily institutionalized within the Army if such course of action became desirable.

The cost data for each unit in the force was derived from the Army's Force Cost Information System (FCIS), with the exception of the costs of wartime active replacement and ammunition for purposes other than training.

FCIS can provide data aggregated at various levels, e.g., battalion, company, platoon/team, etc. For our purposes, data was obtained at both the company and the platoon/team levels for all units in the notional corps. The FCIS provides investment, MPA and OMA costs, both non-recurring and recurring, for all cost elements included in each of the appropriation categories. In addition, it includes the non-recurring investment costs (procurement appropriations) of all major line item number (LIN) items of equipment for that unit. MPA costs were calculated on the basis of military occupational specialty (MOS). Total quantity of personnel is provided by officers, enlisted men, and civilians.

All non-recurring investment costs in the combat force cost projection analysis technique were distributed to the functional group to which each pertained. Recurring investment costs were correspondingly related to the same functional groups.

To distribute MPA costs by functional groups, recourse was made to the specific Table of Organization and Equipment (TO&E) for the unit. OMA costs were distributed to functional groups of systems in accordance with categories previously established by the distribution of investment and MPA costs.

While the FCIS includes the cost of ammunition for training purposes, it does not include the cost of ammunition reserves. Ammunition reserve quantities were obtained by BSI from the Army Concepts Analysis Agency and costed using pricing information provided by DCSRDA/DCSLOG. Allocation of ammunition costs to units and functional groups was accomplished by relating ammunition to the weapons in such units.

The FCIS also excludes wartime active replacement reserve costs. Depot Systems Command (DESCOM) is the source for this type of data in the Army. Each type of equipment has its own rate.

The concept of the "consumer" is that every unit at the company level or lower can be assigned to a consumer category which is selected on the basis of the principal reason for the existence of the unit. Using the army standard capability categories functional group of systems to define consumers, there are thirty-nine possible consumers. A tank platoon comes under the category "Tank;" a medical company falls under "Medical;" a combat engineer company falls under "Combat Engineering," and so forth.

When the "assignment" to a consumer category is made for any individual unit, all costs of that unit in all functional groups of systems are automatically accounted for in that consumer category.

By proceeding in this fashion, it is possible to identify the costs for directly related activities which are required by the principal activities of the military unit. For instance, one can tell that for every dollar spent directly on tanks in the tank consumer column in the notional corps, an additional $1.12 is spent indirectly for other functional groups in the tank consumer column; and that supply and transportation and maintenance account for nearly half of that additional amount. Obviously, a piece of equipment does not stand alone but acts as a consumer supported by other systems. The tank requires personnel to operate it; it expends ammunition; it must be maintained; it requires night observation equipment and tactical communications, and the list goes on. There are also secondary or indirect costs, for example, the vehicles that maintain the tank. Those supporting vehicles also require maintenance themselves, creating induced costs.

The initial assignment of units and unit costs to consumer categories was first accomplished using the notional armored division. All thirty-nine of the army standard capability categories were established as potential consumer categories. In assignment of every armored division piece of equipment made, as it turned out, only sixteen of the thirty-nine possible consumer categories were used. The other twenty-three did not appear, either because no divisional equipment was primarily dedicated to any of such categories of activity, (such as medium or long range air defense) or because the categories, by their very nature, could not represent the primary activities of any military unit (such as night observation or training devices).

Within the total group of sixteen consumer categories, moreover, it was noted that only seven represented what might be considered primary military activities, whereas the remaining nine existed only to support the personnel or activities represented by the primary military activities. In recognition of this fact, a method for allocating the costs of the remaining nine against the seven primary consumer categories was developed. The seven primary consumers and the nine secondary consumers in the notional armored division as well as the percent of total costs for a twenty-year life cycle are shown in Chart 9. The primary consumers are 57% of the total twenty year life cycle cost of $7.7 billion. Note that the important anti-tank group of systems consumes only two percent of total costs.

At the total corps level, the number of total consumers came to twenty-one, while the primary consumers totaled ten. The corps mission responsibilities

Chart 9

CONSUMERS
NOTIONAL ARMORED DIVISION

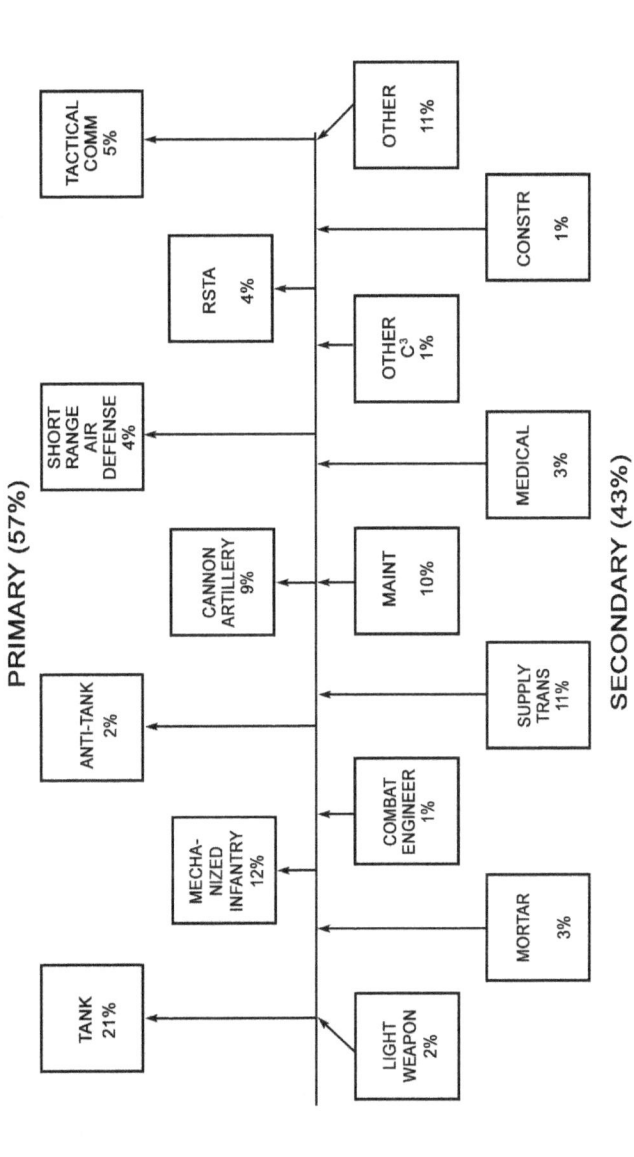

PRIMARY (57%)

- TANK 21%
- MECHA-NIZED INFANTRY 12%
- ANTI-TANK 2%
- CANNON ARTILLERY 9%
- SHORT RANGE AIR DEFENSE 4%
- RSTA 4%
- TACTICAL COMM 5%

SECONDARY (43%)

- LIGHT WEAPON 2%
- MORTAR 3%
- COMBAT ENGINEER 1%
- SUPPLY TRANS 11%
- MAINT 10%
- MEDICAL 3%
- OTHER C^3 1%
- CONSTR 1%
- OTHER 11%

Source: Office of Battlefield Systems Integration/MITRE, 1977

required the addition of three primary consumers in addition to the seven in the division, which were Rockets/Missiles, Medium Range AD and EW. The matrix of the cost categories for the 20-year notionals by missions areas and functional groups of systems versus appropriation categories for all consumers shown at Chart 10 provides a wealth of information. For example, note that in the combat service support mission area the recurring MPA costs of $8.06 billion are more than double the close combat mission area recurring MPA costs of $3.696 billion, and that fire support ammunition costs of $2.313 billion are almost double the close combat non-recurring investment costs. The total corps operational costs in 1976 was $40,594 million. The costs of the ten primary corps functional groups of systems are displayed at Chart 11 where again several factors jump out at you. First, the huge costs of supply and transportation and maintenance. In the "tooth to tail" analogy, the tail seems to "wag" the cost dog. With respect to maintenance, the MPA costs are seven times investment costs. Obviously, there are many offset possibilities: an increase in maintenance procurement, say for diagnostic equipment, could reduce the requirement for maintenance personnel; perhaps the requirement for the manufacturer to meet the "mean time between failure" criteria was not stringent enough; equipment operators could be poorly trained requiring more maintenance; or the equipment design was so complex that maintenance requirements were high. Unquestionably, the man-machine interface is of prime importance.

Tactical communications are also manpower-intensive. The TOE of signal units should be carefully scrutinized. Modern communications equipment will do away with the maintenance efforts to string wired communications, for example. The investment in RSTA is about one-tenth the cost of ammunition. Improved target acquisition would definitely reduce ammo requirements and at the same time greatly improve combat effectiveness. Terminally guided munitions, although very expensive, would still reduce the cost of conducting area coverage firings.

The total costs by the primary consumers in the notional corps and armored and mechanized infantry divisions varied only slightly and as expected, about one third of the divisional costs go to support the tank and mechanized infantry functional systems, which are the main units that inflict damage upon the enemy. What astounded me was the fact that in the notional corps the costs of cannon artillery ($4.12B) exceeded mechanized infantry ($3.67B) and was almost as large as tank costs ($4.71B). The functions of locating the enemy (ISTA) and bringing fire to

Chart 10

NOTIONAL CORP COST CATEGORIES

8 SEPT 1977

FUNCTIONAL GROUP	N/R INV	AMMO	RESV	REC INV	TOTAL INV	N/R MPA	REC MPA	TOTAL MPA	N/R OMA	REC OMA	TOTAL OMA	TOTAL N/R	TOTAL REC	TOTAL
CLOSE COMBAT	1299193	196826	402888	2632844	4531752	97322	3696341	3793663	48284	2034973	2083256	2045510	8364166	10408679
TANK	821077	123658	258504	1333940	2537176	28431	1076820	1105251	13898	1057540	1071438	1245565	3468300	4713865
MECH INF	176470	0	52464	492419	721353	51553	2124147	2175697	19865	750299	770164	300352	3366863	3667215
ANTI-TANK	205923	50107	54123	242020	552183	14418	367660	382078	13420	201600	215020	338001	811280	1149279
CST AVIATION		681	0	0	681	0	0	0	0	0	0	681	0	681
LIGHT WEAPON	95727	22681	37787	564469	720364	2920	127719	130639	1101	25540	26641	159916	717728	877644
FIRE SUPPORT	288067	2313140	35958	444840	3082009	39171	1776237	1816409	20558	741600	762158	2696899	2962674	5659574
MORTARS	44686	90344	9006	79480	223516	13261	533420	546681	6152	225320	231472	163449	838220	1001669
CANNON ARTY	224235	2168556	19866	355020	2767677	18832	916920	935752	10142	405600	415742	2441628	1677537	4119167
ROCKET/RSELS	13128	54249	5805	4400	77642	650	27340	27990	389	6080	6469	74281	37820	112101
FIRE SPT SPT	6018	0	1221	5940	13179	6428	298557	304985	3875	104600	108475	17542	409100	426642
OTHER CBT SPT	151325	2226	27392	85320	266263	14166	552319	566485	6903	195600	202503	202012	833239	1035251
NIGHT OBSERV	106764	0	14824	53300	174887	3096	68400	71496	738	37080	37818	125421	158780	284201
COMBAT ENGNR	31079	2226	7154	28100	68559	4344	204080	208424	3416	72460	75876	48219	304639	352858
MINE/CTRMINE	442	0	98	240	780	6	400	406	4	80	84	550	720	1270
NBC	10156	0	5316	1140	16612	2471	74920	77391	785	22720	23505	18728	98780	117507
CBT SPT SPT	2885	0	0	2540	5425	4249	204520	208769	1960	63260	65220	9094	270320	279413
AIR OFFENSE	244658	143904	22361	221680	632603	14190	512600	526790	9112	370840	379952	434225	1105118	1539342
SHORT RNG AO	185248	104593	22312	172660	484813	10391	380340	390731	6409	310260	316669	328953	863260	1192211
MED RNG AO	59002	39311	48	48540	146901	3236	112820	116056	2491	55880	58371	104088	217240	321328
LONG RNG AO			1	480	481	563	19440	20003	212	4700	4912	776	24620	25396
AIR OFF SPT	408				408							408		408
CBT SVC SPT	1030258		103378	1063424	2197060	205727	8050292	8256019	142341	2783128	2925469	1479545	11906852	13386395
SUPPLY/TRANS	760375		78430	824845	1663650	88337	3670940	3759284	66671	1434302	1500977	993812	5930095	6929307
MAINTENANCE	205588		20885	178519	404992	74373	2789934	2862309	41037	935750	976787	341882	3902204	4244085
MEDICAL	11832		1596	13380	26808	29115	1210755	1239870	29780	310998	340778	72323	1535133	1607455
ENERGY	46615		1429	34780	82824	1616	74800	76415	1413	24080	25493	51073	133659	184732
AVIATION SPT	3080		71	2180	5331	1063	35920	36983	1150	12080	13230	5364	50180	55544
OTHER C S S	2770		967	9720	13457	9068	279939	289007	2291	65920	68211	15096	355579	370675
ISTA	183496		20457	158280	362232	32321	1157238	1189558	22579	451199	473778	258852	1766716	2025569
RSTA	109162		19193	97000	225355	22861	833939	856799	16065	345659	361724	167281	1276597	1443876
SIGINT	2035		0	1680	3715	641	19620	20261	312	5340	5652	2988	26640	29628
EW	64979		1053	49660	115692	3063	82720	85783	3676	37460	41136	72771	169840	242611
STRTGS INTEL						52	2900	2952	26	580	606	78	3480	3558
INTEL SPT	7320		211	9940	17471	5704	218060	223764	2500	62160	64660	15735	290160	305895
CMD SYSTEMS	104739		34879	83180	222797	42120	1613009	1655129	18056	515397	533452	199793	2211585	2411376
POSITION LOC														
STRTGS COMM	79162		21654	78540	179355	41151	1563869	1605020	17611	498957	516567	159577	2141365	2300942
TACTICAL COMM	21080		1532	980	23592	80	3680	3760	58	1240	1298	22750	5900	28650
CONSEC	4497		49	3660	8206	889	45460	46349	387	15200	15587	5822	64320	70142
AUTOMATION						0	0	0	0	0	0			0
OTHER C-CUBEC			11644		11644							11644		11644
OTHR SUPPORT	99216		9844	154239	263299	62976	2954488	3017465	34719	812569	847288	206755	3921297	4128053
FIX WING A/C	935		21	1060	2016	15	755	755	31	320	351	1002	2120	3122
ADMIN VEHCLS	36642		5092	53740	95474	12428	507639	520067	6624	161660	168283	60786	723039	783825
CONSTRUCTION	61639		4731	99439	163809	50533	2446111	2496643	28064	650589	678653	144967	3196138	3341106
OTHER														
TRAINING DEV														
TOTAL	3400937	2656103	657155	4843791	11558002	505836	20322464	20828320	302552	7905291	8207843	7522577	33071472	40594080

DOLLARS IN THOUSANDS

ALL CONSUMERS

Source: Office of Battlefield Systems Integration, 1977

Chart 11

NOTIONAL CORPS 20 YEAR COST DISTRIBUTION
BY
FUNCTIONAL GROUPS OF SYSTEMS
($ MILLIONS)

FUNCTIONAL GROUPS OF SYSTEMS	TOTAL COSTS	INVESTMENT	MPA	OMP	AMMO
SUPPLY AND TRANSPORTATION	6924	1664	3759	1501	-
TANK	4714	2414	1105	1071	124
MAINTENANCE	4244	405	2862	977	-
CANNON ARTILLERY	4119	599	936	416	2169
MECH INFANTRY	3667	721	2176	770	-
TACTICAL COMMUNICATIONS	2301	179	1605	517	-
MEDICAL	1608	27	1240	341	-
RECON/SURV/TGT ACQ	1444	225	857	362	-
SHORT RANGE AIR DEFENSE	1192	380	391	317	105
ANTI-TANK	1149	502	382	215	50
SUBTOTAL	31362	7116	15313	6487	2448
TOTAL	40594	8902	20828	8208	2656

Source: Office of Battlefield Systems Integration/MITRE, 1977

bear (tactical communications) can reduce the costs of artillery and they need to be emphasized not only for that reason but also for the functions of commanding and maneuvering forces. It was questionable whether sufficient emphasis was being placed on those two important functions. We will show that to defeat the enemy in Central Europe, NATO forces must be able to attrit enemy second echelon troops as they attempt to reinforce the battle and cannon artillery would be essential for interdiction fires. However, a question for today is, "In a limited war environment is the past heavy reliance on artillery prudent?".

The information determined by the Input-Output analysis can be displayed in many meaningful formats and in great detail. Interestingly, the general breakdown of categories of costs for the notional corps, armored division, and mechanized division, were about the same. Table 4 shows the categories of costs by budget appropriation for a notional armored division for both a ten and twenty year life cycle.

Table 4
Total Cost Distribution for Notional Armored Corps or Division
By Budget Appropriations in Percent

	Twenty Year	Ten Year
Investment	29	40
Military Personnel	50	42
Operations & Maintenance	21	18
Non-Recurring	20	34
Recurring	80	66

Generally speaking, most major pieces of equipment remain in inventory for about twenty years unless there has been a major technical breakthrough. Note then that personnel costs are 50% of the twenty year life cycle costs and investments are 29%. Procurement costs always loom large initially and generally drive the debate on which system and how many items to procure. However, looking at the breakdown of investment costs in Table 5 which follows you can see that non-recurring initial procurement costs are only 8% of the total twenty year life cycle costs. Decision makers who generally focus upon the initial non-recurring investment costs of equipment would do well to more closely consider life-cycle costs.

Table 5
Investment Cost Distribution for Notional Armored Corps or Division
By Budget Appropriation in Percent

Twenty Year Life Cycle

INVESTMENT	29
• Non-recurring	(8)
• Ammunition	(7)
• Reserve	(2)
• Twenty-Year Recurring	(12)

Furthermore, the operations and support costs as a percentage of total costs are 88.7%, defined as recurring costs divided by total costs minus war reserves (ammo and equipment). The Army's funding on a life cycle basis goes into pay and allowances, training, operating costs, maintenance and supply activities. Although the spotlight of interest is predominantly focused on procurement, the factors of training, manning, and operations are vital and not enough consideration has been given to potential trade-offs between the procurement of equipment and its operations. Much more attention must be given to reducing the large manpower requirements in the combat service support mission area.

The I-O data was developed to help answer cost-related questions with respect to increasing combat effectiveness on the battlefield, such as:

• Which areas are labor intensive and which are capital intensive?
• What are the major cost drivers?
• How do costs of various functions compare with one another, e.g., tank vs. mechanized infantry?
• What are the ratios between different cost categories, e.g., MPA vs. investment?
• How large a percentage of total costs is attributed to supply and transportation?

Our science and technology review resulted in the development of the SPIDER charts which provided a graphical display of the relationships between current operational and future requirements for battlefield systems and the work being done in the Army's R&D laboratories, promoted user/developer dialogue, prioritized requirements and related the technological base to the Army mission areas. The Input-Output cost analysis in a broad sense indicated where the Army's funding was being utilized with respect to fielded combat units. These two studies, while sharpening our insights, did not answer the "Equipment Challenge":

What do we need?
What can we afford?

These two questions were both a function of cost and combat effectiveness. To determine combat effectiveness, a thorough analysis of enemy capabilities was necessary. In 1976, the major threat to the US and to NATO was the Warsaw Pact. Therefore, we had to analyze the Soviet equipment, tactics, capabilities, and vulnerabilities. Only then could a final battlefield system architecture be completed by measuring weapons effectiveness against the enemy.

THE THREAT

Our Armed Forces must have the capabilities to effectively operate in a broad spectrum of combat situations, from counterinsurgency to all-out war. In 1975, the Warsaw Pact forces in Central Europe were the major threat to US and world stability, and it may be so today. Consequently, at the time BSI focused attention on countering that threat.

Senators Nunn and Bartlett's report of 24 January 1977, NATO and the New Soviet Threat, summed up the prevailing opinions of the times when it stated[1]:

> "It is the central thesis of this report that the Soviet Union and its European allies are rapidly moving towards a decisive conventional military superiority over NATO... Soviet conventional forces in Europe have undergone significant expansion during the past decade and are now being qualitatively improved."

At the time, it was substantially agreed that there was a "declining credibility of nuclear responses to non-nuclear aggression," so our threat analysis focused primarily upon conventional warfare.

It was very important, therefore, to study the qualitative and quantitative improvements to the Soviet forces, which at the time were primarily those of the Warsaw Pact facing NATO forces in Central Europe. Subsequently, an analysis of Soviet tactical concepts would enable a war gaming scenario to be utilized which, as you will see, will highlight Soviet vulnerabilities enabling us to recommend future developmental objectives. BSI was ably assisted in our threat analysis by Mr. J. V. Braddock and the BDM Corporation.

During the decade of US involvement in Vietnam, the Soviets made many important qualitative improvements to their combat equipment. Our foreign intelligence system did an excellent job keeping our equipment developers aware of developments in the Soviet arsenal. We received timely information from the Foreign Science and Technology Center, the Missile Intelligence Agency, the Assistant Chief of Staff for Intelligence, and local foreign intelligence offices where the mission was to prevent any potential technology surprises and to assist in insuring that we developed superior battlefield equipment to counter the enemy[2].

Soviet doctrine called for massive deep armor penetrations by armored and motorized rifle divisions, putting a premium on tanks, armored personnel carriers, reconnaissance and infantry combat vehicles, artillery, and multiple rocket launchers and air defense.

The following Soviet ground combat systems which had been introduced in the 1960's and 70's provided Soviet Ground Forces with a qualitative advantage over comparable American systems[2].

Tank   The T-72 medium main battle tank was introduced in 1973. It weighed 35 tons, had a 115-125 mm gun with an automatic loading system, a laser-range finder and night observation device. Soviet tank development placed more emphasis on firepower and mobility rather than survivability. Although the main battle tanks were quite well armored, they were vulnerable to 105 armor piercing rounds up to 1000 meters, with the major vulnerability in the external fuel tanks and in the ammo storage.

Infantry Combat Vehicle   The tracked BMP was introduced in 1967. Weighing 14 tons, it had a 73 mm gun with an AT SAGGER missile launcher on top of the gun tube. It had a crew of three and carried eight light infantrymen who were able to fight from the vehicle without dismounting. The US at the time had no ICV.

Reconnaissance Vehicle   The BRDM-2, a wheeled vehicle weighing 7 tons, capable of speeds of 60 MPH, was fielded in 1966. It is armed with a 14.5 mm machine gun and is outfitted with a SAGGER missile. At the time, we had no mounted ATGMs.

Artillery   The Soviets introduced the M 1973 Self-Propelled gun in 1974. Prior to its introduction, which permitted artillery to keep pace with advancing armor, the Soviet field guns were all towed. Towed guns are light and simple and can be brought into action quickly, but they lack cross-country mobility and have no gun crew protection against counter-battery fires. The M-46 130 mm gun has a range of 27,000 meters and the modern and versatile 122 mm D-30 howitzer, the Soviet's basic artillery piece, has a range of 15,000 meters. Soviet weapons generally out-ranged the US counterparts.

Multiple Rocket Launchers The BM-21, the latest multi-barreled rocket launcher, introduced in 1964, was a major step forward in providing the Soviets the capability to deliver crushing artillery strikes at decisive moments in a battle. Each launcher delivers a 40 round salvo in less than 30 seconds. Reloading took about 10 minutes, however, a Czech version could load a second salvo in a minute. At the time, the US did not have a multiple rocket launcher.

Air Defense The Soviet ground forces had a formidable array of tactical air defense weapons. The ZSU-23-4 is an outstanding gun system which was introduced in 1965. This self-propelled gun has an on-board radar and an optimum range of 2500-3000 meters. It is very effective against close support tactical aircraft. The SA-6 track-mounted missile system was fielded in 1967. It is powered by a solid rocket ramjet system and is command guided by a fire control radar. It has a slant range of about 30 kilometers.

Aircraft The Soviets also introduced the HIND helicopter in 1972, and a new series of tactical aircraft, such as the FOXBAT in 1971. However, with regard to aircraft, US technology was still superior.

Obviously, all the new Soviet combat systems had not replaced the older models in the hands of troops. It will take years, for example, for the new T-72 main battle tank to replace the thousands of older T-62 and T-55 tanks. Yet, as these new systems are fielded over time they will provide the Soviets with a quantitative as well as qualitative advantage.

Quantitatively, the Soviets surpassed the US in all major categories of conventional weapons except helicopters. Soviet personnel strengths were at least two and a half times those of the US, and they had about 168 divisions compared to a US total of 19. The Soviets' 40,000 main battle tanks compared to the US 10,000, and their available anti-tank guided missiles were three times ours. A comparison of the quantity of equipment is shown on Chart 12.

Equipment of itself does not determine the outcome of battles. There are many other considerations, such as training, leadership, morale, command and control, and combat experience. All these factors must be considered. In particular, the US has long had the advantage of technological supremacy in such areas as computers, guidance systems, night vision, electronic counter measures, target acquisition, artillery ammunition, and guided munitions. These strengths can be harnessed to provide meaningful force multipliers.

Chart 12

THE SOVIET THREAT

COMPARISON: QUANTITY OF EQUIPMENT

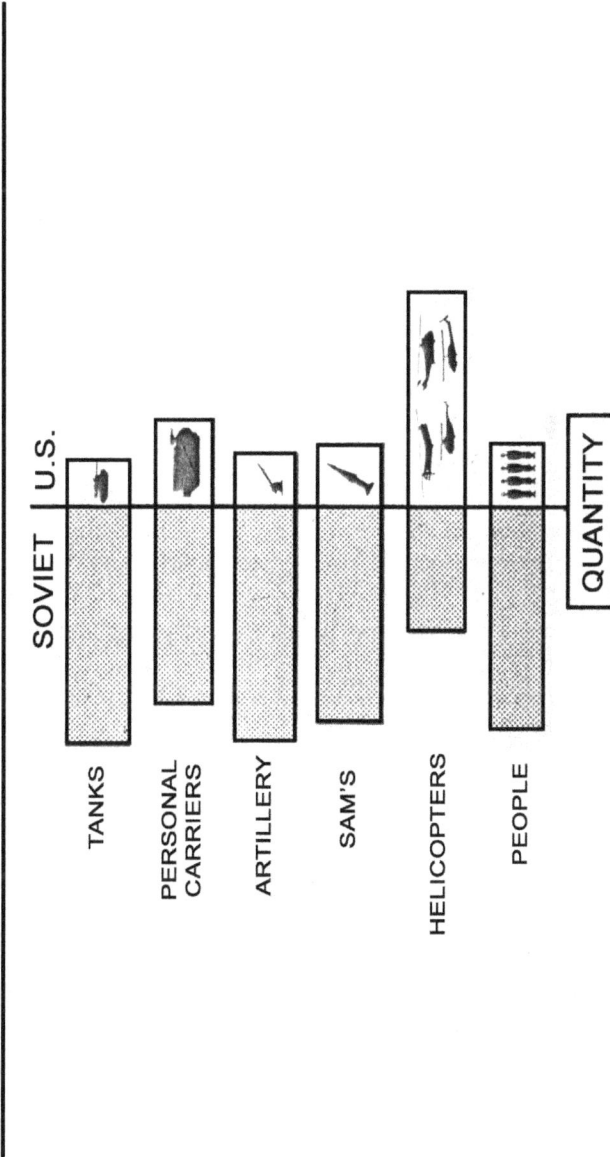

SOVIET | U.S.

TANKS

PERSONAL CARRIERS

ARTILLERY

SAM'S

HELICOPTERS

PEOPLE

QUANTITY

Source: Office of Battlefield Systems Integration/Foreign Service and Technology Center, 1976

We had been told that the Soviets are technically inferior, that they are inflexible and cannot adopt to changing combat situations, that their conscripted troops do not have the training necessary to be effective, that they have language problems, that they don't have an essential logistic support capability, and finally that the soldiers have low morale. These reports may or may not be true, but the fact is that the Soviets had the doctrine, organization, and equipment necessary to conduct combat operations, and they were a formidable threat to NATO and US forces in Europe. It was essential for the US to develop the modern equipment required to defeat the Soviets and to accomplish this in a cost effective, balanced manner. To do that, it was necessary to fully understand Soviet tactical doctrine.

Soviet tactical doctrine stated that decisive results are achieved only through offensive action. They stress the concentration of force (mass), surprise and maneuver. An offensive would probably begin with a massive artillery and air neutralization of the enemy defenses, particularly the ATGMs, followed by a simultaneous attack on several axes along a broad front. The initial threats would be intended to break through the enemy defense to enable highly mobile units to exploit the breakthrough to seize deep objectives and to encircle and destroy the enemy forces. Motorized rifle troops are considered the basic and most versatile arm of the Soviet armed forces, and they are seldom employed without strong artillery, tank, and engineer support. Tanks are employed at all echelons, and their principal role is, by shock action, to be the exploitation force. Considering the terrain of Eastern Germany and NATO defenses, the Soviets believe that the rate of advance for their breakthrough phase must be 20 to 40 kilometers per day and the exploitation phase double that amount. To achieve these results, the ratio of combat power must be 3:1 infantry, 5:1 tanks, and about 10:1 artillery. These ratios compare with Soviet experiences in World War II, and the above rates of advance are only double World War II experiences when the troops traveled on foot.

The design of their ground force units facilitated the dual concepts of mass and maneuver. Maintenance of the momentum of attack was considered critical. To do this, advancing troops bypass or envelop strongly held areas, particularly built-up areas. The army normally attacks in two echelons with the lead echelon attacking in parallel division columns preceded by strong advanced elements, greatly augmented with artillery and anti-tank weapons. The second echelon usually follows about 30 to 40 kilometers behind the lead echelon.

The Soviets envisioned two types of attack: the classic deliberate breakthrough and the meeting engagement. Deployment in both attacks is from the line of march. The meeting engagement is perceived as the most common offensive action and occurs when one of the combatants meets the enemy unexpectedly. It is characterized by a rapidly changing situation, and the Soviets believe that success is obtained through a rapid concentration of forces and aggressive action despite the lack of knowledge of enemy dispositions. Soviet Colonel I. Konyushenke, writing in the Red Star on 17 March 1976, states[3],

> "It is understandable that the achievement of victory in such a battle is possible for the commander who deeply understands the nature of modern battle. Here the art, the flexibility of tactical thinking of the commander sometimes plays a decisive role in assuring success."

This brings us to a discussion of the Soviet philosophy of command. Commanders have full responsibility for every aspect of activities under their control. Consequently, aware of such responsibilities, they do not usually utilize their staff to the fullest. Soviet staff procedures themselves are cumbersome and wasteful. Plans are rigid and detailed, limiting unit and individual initiatives. This results in slow reactions to unforeseen circumstances such as in a meeting engagement.

Surprise is another major tactical principle and is an important element in seizing the offense. Surprise is augmented through cover and deception. Cover is obtained by use of camouflage, movement at night and in inclement weather, and by smoke. The use of smoke appears more and more in Soviet papers and it could cause major degradation of our ATGMs. The Soviet Military Herald, in January 1975, stated[4],

> "Smoke screens are finding increasing application in military training. They ensure screening of troops from enemy optical, television, infrared, and laser reconnaissance instruments, and produce disturbances in the work of gun laying systems. This creates favorable conditions for executing combat missions with smaller losses."

In the attack, the artillery units required for the Soviets' massive preparatory fires are the first combat units to deploy. Current planning calls for over 100 guns per kilometer in the breakthrough sector, meaning that about 500 guns may be deployed to support a Soviet division. Such artillery movements when detected provide a target-rich environment for counter-fires, but the US requires longer range artillery systems and improved munitions to be really effective. The addition of multiple rocket launchers has greatly increased the suppressive capabilities of Soviet artillery.

The severe tank losses in the 1973 Yom Kippur War from ATGMs did not go unnoticed by the Soviets. They greatly increased the number of ATGMs in their divisions so that they have several times as many as does the US. Since the main battle tank remains the decisive tactical weapon in the central duel of combat, it is incumbent on the US to improve the armor protection of a new tank to defeat the ATGMs and thus insure battlefield survivability. So concerned are the Soviets over the ATGM potential to destroy tanks that their priorities of engagement for tank gunners are: ATGMs, tanks, and anti-tank guns in that order[5].

As mentioned, the Soviets envisaged two types of attack: a meeting engagement or a classic deliberate breakthrough[6]. In either case, emphasis is on preemptive maneuvers as indicated in Chart 13. Both the motorized rifle division and the tank division are highly mobile and have over 500 tracked vehicles and about 1,700 wheeled vehicles.

Table 6
Enemy Vulnerabilities
Mobility

Equipment	Tank Division	Motorized Division
TANK	344	306
APC	177	313
ARTY	60	72
MISSILES	22	22
TRUCK	1686	1819

They normally attack in two or more echelons and will maneuver on multiple axes attempting to achieve a rapid concentration of weapons while carrying out the attack with daring thrusts. Normally, the divisions will deploy for combat from march formation and that requires great road space and <u>time</u>.

Chart 13

SOVIET TACTICS

EMPHASIS ON PRE-EMPTIVE MANEUVER

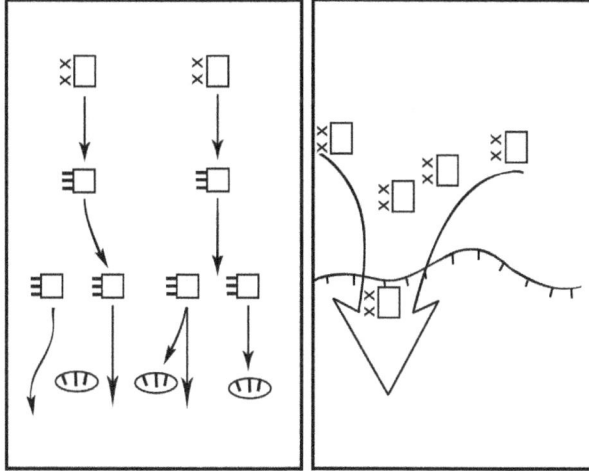

MEETING ENGAGEMENT

- GRANUALAR DEFENSE
- DARING THRUSTS
- MANEUVER ON MULTIPLE AXES
- REGIMENTAL LEVEL

CLASSIC BREAKTHROUGH

- LINEAR DEFENSE
- MASS FOR ATTACK
- CONCENTRATED FIREPOWER
- DIVISION/ARMY LEVEL

Source: Department of Army Publications, Military Operations of the Soviet Army, 1976

The tank division is the primary maneuver element and it may be employed in either the first or second echelon. In either case its mission is to exploit gaps in the enemy defenses by violent and aggressive offensive operations. Its attack zone varies between 5-12 kilometers and it normally advances in multiple columns with tracked vehicles moving cross-country and the wheeled vehicles on roads. The division will always employ an advanced guard, usually a reinforced tank battalion with reconnaissance elements, engineer and artillery and air defense support. Chart 14 shows the distance factors of a tank division in a meeting engagement. It is advancing on one major axis but with three columns. The point elements of the advanced guard are 30 kilometers ahead of the main body lead regiment. From front to rear the tank division is spread out over 80 kilometers. Upon meeting the enemy, all elements must close as rapidly as possible. Again, the key to Soviet doctrine is to maintain <u>momentum</u>, which is defined by the MASS times VELOCITY. They recognize that vulnerability increases greatly as they mass. However, vulnerability is also reduced with increased velocity of movement. Thus, the trade-off to maintain momentum (see Chart 15). A tank division in a meeting engagement could have its second echelon elements take over five hours to deploy in their envelopment efforts and it would take the divisional artillery about four hours for a full buildup. In a typical classic breakthrough with two tank divisions echeloned in depth to maintain momentum in continuous combat, it would take between 14 and 20 hours for the second echelon division to deploy along the FEBA. Soviet dispositions at the time of initial contact for both the classic breakthrough and the meeting engagement are such that fifty percent of the Soviet forces are from 40 to 50 kilometers from the FEBA and the tail of the columns could be from 60 to 100 kilometers from the FEBA. In a typical classic breakthrough, it could take as long as a day for the second echelon forces to close and there would be additional echelons closely following it in order to maintain momentum. Soviet offensive doctrine requires that the attack be conducted continuously "night and day without let-up until the enemy is defeated"[7].

Chart 14

DISTANCE FACTORS

MEETING ENGAGEMENT
SOVIET PERCEPTION TANK DIVISION

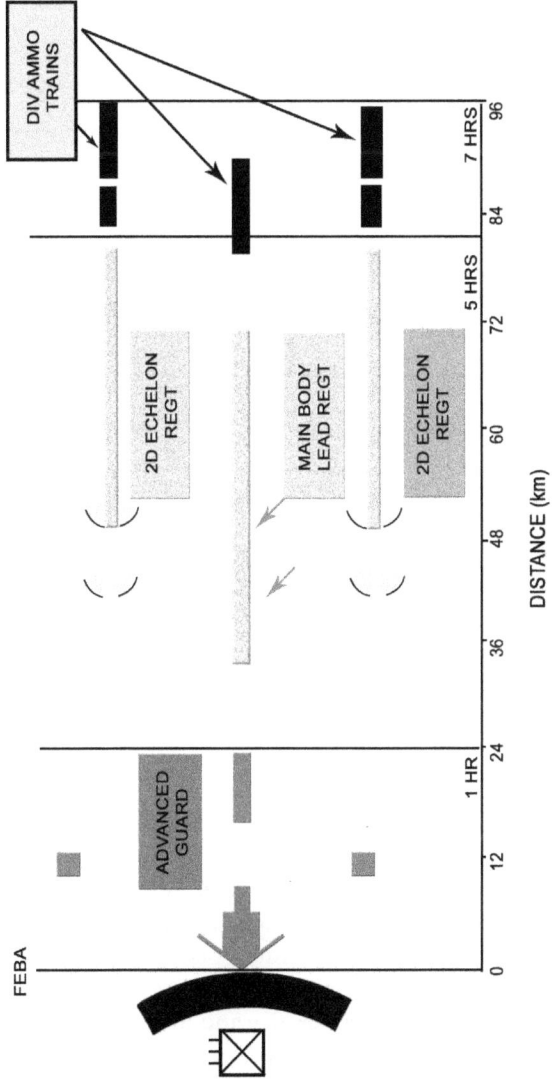

DIV AMMO TRAINS

7 HRS

5 HRS

2D ECHELON REGT

MAIN BODY LEAD REGT

2D ECHELON REGT

1 HR

ADVANCED GUARD

FEBA

0   12   24   36   48   60   72   84   96

DISTANCE (km)

Source: BDM, Dept. Of Army Publication, Manual on Soviet Army Operations, 1976

61

The Soviet time-distance factors are summarized in the following table.

Table 7
Summary of Soviet Time-Distance Factors

TACTIC	TAIL OF COLUMN FROM FEBA	TIME	
		Preparation	Committed
MEETING ENGAGEMENT (DIV)	60-140 km	0	4-7 Hrs
CLASSIC BREAKTHROUGH (2 DIV)	60-80 km	24-48 Hrs	5-12 Hrs (1st Div) 5-24 Hrs (2nd Div)

The large number of soviet tanks and vehicles spread out over such large distances creates a <u>major Soviet vulnerability</u>.

As stated previously, the Soviets had adopted the Napoleonic credo of momentum, that is, mass times velocity (see Chart 15). It is at the FEBA, the location of the central duel, that the Soviet attack velocity has slowed and its troops are massed. It is there that we must (1) destroy his massed troops with firepower, and (2) reinforce our defenses at the critical point. As his second echelon units hurry to concentrate force at the decisive battle ongoing at the FEBA, we must also (3) attrit those forces and impede their velocity of advance. These three actions are the key to victory.

Analysis of the past several hundred years of battles indicates that weapons lethality has increased inexorably over time. On the other hand, the intensity of battle decreased, reaching a low point in World War I with its defensive trench warfare resulting in battles of long duration. However, since World War I, the intensity of combat has greatly increased. Modern battle is characterized by violent and aggressive action, high attrition rates, and continuous all-weather, day and night combat which results in decisive engagements of short duration. In such battles, the combat intensity is very high when first engaged and declines rapidly thereafter over time. For troops on the defensive it is essential that they slow the battle tempo.

Chart 15

SECOND ECHELON ATTACK

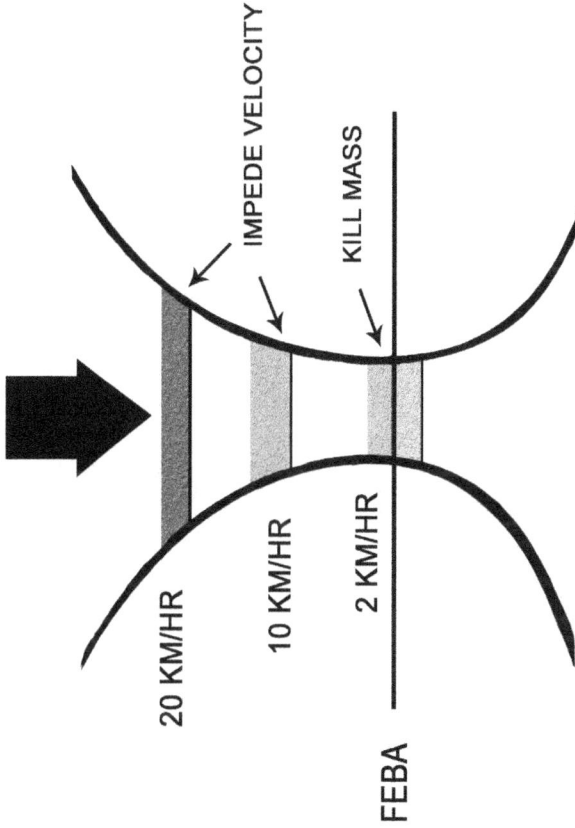

IMPEDE VELOCITY

KILL MASS

20 KM/HR

10 KM/HR

2 KM/HR

FEBA

MOMENTUM = MASS x VELOCITY

Source: Office of Battelfield Systems Integration, 1977

The necessity to attrit second echelon troops tens of kilometers from the FEBA means that tactical air force support is absolutely vital, not only to impede the enemy rear echelon, but to assist in the destruction of the enemy at the main battle area by close air support. The Air Force must be fully integrated into all combat analyses.

To summarize, Soviet offensive tactical doctrine required[8]:

- Surprise
- Concentration of Forces
- Bold Armor Thrusts
- Destruction of Enemy Air
- Momentum

In 1976 the Soviets had:

- Concepts
- Modern Equipment
- Numbers

and
- VULNERABILITIES

It was the goal of our battlefield system architecture to provide a method for developing, evaluating, and integrating battlefield systems to maximize the combat capabilities of US forces against any potential adversary. With respect to Central Europe, we had to take advantage of Soviet vulnerabilities, thereby assuring victory should a conflict arise.

When considering the threat the principals of warfare remain invariant, however in the every-changing world of diplomacy, alliances and power politics it is not unusual that one's potential enemies are subject to change. During WWII Russia was a strong ally of the United States in the common cause to defeat Nazi Germany. In 1945 as a young lieutenant stationed in Germany helping to rebuild the war torn devastated infrastructure I would never have believed that some thirty years later I would be one of five US general officers meeting with five senior German generals in a huge chilly Gobelian tapestried hall in a Bavarian castle discussing the Air-Land Battle and methods to stop a potential Soviet offensive against NATO forces[9].

When fighting outnumbered, as in Central Europe, it is important to reduce the intensity of battle. Battle intensity is a function of the combat losses.

In the modern era intensity is generally greatest at the beginning of the battle, and the intensity tapers off in the duration of the battle. Friendly losses can be reduced by improving the survivability of our own weapons. The tempo of the battle can be slowed by suppressing the enemy through interdiction, mine fields, EW, and smoke. The selective degradation of enemy command and control is vital, and the importance of slowing the enemy reinforcements cannot be overestimated.

The two major vulnerabilities of the Soviets were command and control and mobility and these will be discussed subsequently. In 1976 many scenarios depicting a NATO conflict with Warsaw Pact forces in Central Europe were available and were of great value in developing, evaluating, and integrating battlefield systems to take advantage of the vulnerabilities of the potential adversary.

Our threat analysis concluded that to obtain a favorable force ratio we had to:

1)   Attrit the enemy engaged in the central duel where he is MASSED.

2)   Attrit and impede enemy reinforcements by slowing down his VELOCITY of advance.

3)   Reinforce the central duel with our own units through excellent ISTA and C&C.

The aforementioned three actions required to obtain a favorable relative force ratio (F) can be summarized in a simplistic formula.

$$\text{Equation 1:} \quad F = \frac{Bo + Br - Ba}{Ro + Rr - Ra}$$

Where: Bo, Ro are the initial force strengths of <u>engaged</u> Blue and Red forces

      Br, Rr are the strengths of reinforcements to the main battle area,

      Ba, Ra are the attrition of forces in the main battle area, the central duel.

It is obvious that to obtain a favorable Blue force ratio that Blue must maximize his reinforcements less attrition (Br - Ba) and at the same time minimizing Red's reinforcements while maximizing Red attrition (Rr - Ra). The subjects of Zone 2 attrition and reinforcements will be discussed later.(Page 91)

The relative force ratio is an important factor in determining the relative combat power of opposing forces which determines the output of battles. Other factors are the situation, which includes offense or defense, the terrain, weather, etc., and the relative weapons lethality. The overall weapons lethality is a function of the summation of the measures of combat effectiveness of individual weapons systems and will be discussed subsequently.

MEASURES OF COMBAT EFFECTIVENESS

Having analyzed the most likely near term potential threat, three of the four basic architectural building blocks have been discussed:

- Technology Base (SPIDER charts)
- Costs (Input-Output Program)
- Threat (Soviet tactics)

The first two building blocks reasonably defined user requirements, science and technology objectives, operational capability requirements, and costs. The threat analysis of enemy capabilities provided insights as to the friendly weapons system capabilities required to defeat the enemy. To determine the relative combat effectiveness of weapons systems we turned to the dynamic modeling of potential combat in Central Europe considering the Soviet threat. In any program to modernize or transform combat systems it is essential to know the potential threat in order to design war game scenarios depicting the various excursions of probable battles.

The fourth architectural requirement was a Measure of Combat Effectiveness for individual weapon systems and the relative value of all systems. Linear analysis considering many different variable attributes of an individual system is of value in determining potential improvements to that system. However, recourse to dynamic modeling is necessary to determine the relative value of one combat system to others.

LINEAR ANALYSIS

To get back to the subject of weapons effectiveness, for years there has been a continuing dialogue between users and developers concerning the desired characteristics of a given weapons system. Generally, a weapon's effectiveness has been determined by a linear equation with varying weights assigned to the various weapons characteristics. A linear analysis is helpful in determining the effects of changing the value of a single variable. Take for example the computation for the artillery weapons effectiveness index (WEI), which is a complex equation with eleven variables, of which the most heavily weighted variable is the fractional coverage. The fractional coverage for calibers of various weapons for the improved conventional munitions (ICM) were found to be several times greater than that of the high explosive (HE) round. In the 1970s, the major improvements to the artillery systems were by enhanced munitions. The importance of the ICM will be covered further in the discussion of dynamic modeling.

Linear analysis has been of value particularly in decisions involving product improvements where the measure of an underline individual system weapons effectiveness index (WEI) is required. That is, the incremental value of improvements to a system. Note in Chart 16 the incremental improvement in the WEI of the M60A3 model tank over the earlier M60A1. This indicates the value of product improvement to existing weapons systems, for once a weapons system has been fielded continuing improvements in weapons effectiveness can be made. Product improvement is an important aspect of weapons procurement. The military cannot afford to continually procure new weapons systems as technology improves. The serviceable life of a major system is generally between ten and twenty years. However, new technology can be retrofitted on existing equipment, thereby improving combat effectiveness usually at much lower costs than fielding a new system. An excellent example was the placing of the TOW on the M-113 chassis (the Improved Tow Vehicle) which provided great improvement in combat power and survivability. Product improvements that could have a high payoff are increasing the velocity of the DRAGON anti-armor system and improving the survivability of the Stand-off Target Acquisition System(SOTAS). Although quantum improvements in weapons effectiveness are normally not available through product improvements, it remains a very cost effective way to incrementally increase the combat power of a single system. However, linear analysis as a method is of little value in determining the relative value of one system to others so that meaningful trade-offs between systems can be considered. In these cases heterogeneous dynamic modeling is required.

Chart 16

WEAPON EFFECTIVENESS

TANK
INCREMENTAL IMPROVEMENTS

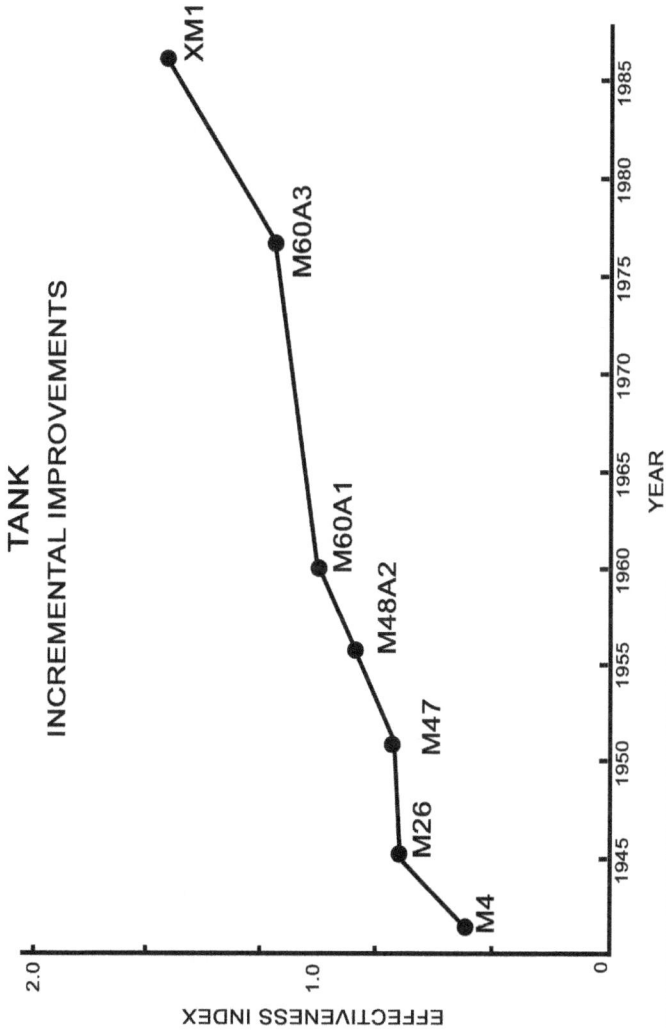

Source: Concept Analysis Group/Tank Special Studies Group, 1976

DYNAMIC MODELING

Heterogeneous dynamic war gaming theory is fairly standard. Dr. Gerald Anderson of my staff working with MITRE, particularly with Charles Joyce and Darrell Penrod, evaluated battle results obtained from many different Army models and war games (IDAGAM, COMCAP, SCORES, and others), generally portraying a Soviet (Red) offensive on European terrain against defensive US (Blue) units, where the Soviets had an initial 3:1 strength advantage. The results of over ninety battles produced by eight different games and models were available and thousands of computer runs were made to obtain averaged values.

A central duel, where the close combat mission area weapons systems are employed, takes place in all war games. The stress of battle measured by attrition is in the central duel. In dynamic modeling, the principal weapons characteristics affecting the outcome of the central duel are firepower and survivability. Mobility is a fundamental aspect of the ability to reinforce the main battle area as well as being able to maneuver (agility) within the battle area. It and other weapons attributes are considered implicitly in the analytical games. A group of experts would labor for weeks in the preparation of a realistic scenario, considering the size of forces, tactics, terrain, and implicit weapons characteristics such as reliability and versatility. Once the combat simulation was programmed, then multiple runs could be made in a matter of minutes, enabling various assumptions to be tested.

In the central duel, only <u>engaged forces</u> contribute to the battle outcome. A weapon's effectiveness is measured by its ability to kill the enemy. Thus the value of a friendly (Blue) weapons system is determined by the number of enemy (Red) systems which it kills. The contributions of all weapons systems engaged in the battle must be considered in determining the effectiveness of any one system. Therefore, if there are B Blue systems and R Red systems there will be 2 BR attrition rates to determine. These attrition rates are then displayed in a matrix form which is called the "killer-victim scoreboard." Blue weapons systems interactions can be displayed versus all Red weapons systems and conversely for Red weapons systems.

The weapons effectiveness value (WEV) of a weapons system on either side is proportional to the rate at which that weapon removes value from the enemy. One weapon is assigned a WEV value of unity (1), in most cases the Blue tank, and all WEVs on either side are determined <u>relatively</u>. The WEV multiplied by the number of engaged systems determines the overall value of the weapon system. The aggregated summation of all Blue systems is the unit effectiveness value (UEV). The ratio of the Blue UEV to the Red UEV is the force effectiveness ratio (FER) which is the battle outcome predictor. The Red and Blue UEVs are an indication of relative combat power, and a force effectiveness ratio greater than one indicates that Blue is the victor.

Once engaged, the battle continues for a given length of time and survival histories are recorded, that is the number of system losses per time interval. At the conclusion, the percent of losses by Blue and Red systems are noted. The percent of losses indicates the stress placed upon a given weapons system. A major goal of any weapons systems improvement would be to reduce the size of the its losses, or for the same losses to increase enemy losses.

In order to analyze the contributions of alternative weapons systems developments it was considered desirable to display several battles in as comparable a fashion as possible and analytic techniques were used to extend the drawdown of forces until the total fraction of Blue armor losses was identical to the base case scenario which would allow the comparison of different battle outcomes.

In order to analyze changes in weapons system designs or the introduction of new weapons systems it was necessary to choose a base case from which different assumptions could be tested. Utilizing the base case, varying assumptions concerning the effectiveness of new systems, increases in various weapons densities and changes in the threat could be run. In the examples that follow, the COMCAP war gaming technique is utilized. This is only one example of many war games.

THE 1977 CENTRAL DUEL

The COMCAP studies performed by the General Research Corporation involved the play of detailed manual computer assisted war games. Much time was spent by qualified tacticians, the human element, to determine the forces, weapons, terrain, and tactics of the war game scenario. The computer then performed the simulations of the details of weapons firing with its many aspects including rate of fire, range, intervisibility, etc., enabling multiple views of the battle to be made in order to obtain meaningful averaged outcomes. In substance, the scenario fed small unit engagements to the combat simulator which produced a killer-victim scoreboard which enabled kill rates and weapons values to be quantified, determining the force effectiveness ratio.

The COMCAP Baseline case pitted the weapons systems in the hands of US and Soviet troops in 1977 with a 3:1 Soviet numerical advantage in an engagement fought on Eastern German terrain. The Blue and Red UEV outcomes were 141.87 and 179.72 respectively, giving a force effectiveness ratio of 0.78943, i.e., Red wins. Chart 17 shows the types and numbers of weapons in each force and the percent of force strength due to each weapon. Note that both Red and Blue forces have fifteen weapons each and the Blue M60A3 tank has been allocated a WEV of 1.00. The killer-victim scoreboard has recorded 450 interactions, each of the fifteen Blue weapons interacting with each of the fifteen Red weapons and vice-versa.

Again, let us consider the tank. Tanks, for example, should be employed in a combined arms operation. It is important that the battle contributions of all weapons systems be considered in determining tank effectiveness. For example, supporting armored vehicles have a great influence on tank design. Armored personnel carriers with ATGMs can provide long range anti-tank capability, and armored personnel carriers with cannons, such as the 73 mm on the BMP, relieve tanks somewhat from the requirement to take on assault targets and suppressive fires. Thus, it is important to note that the tank is one of a family of armored vehicles whose characteristics must be mutually supporting in order to optimize battlefield effectiveness. All close combat systems participate in the central duel and their interactions with enemy and friendly weapons systems are essential to the understanding of the dynamics of the battlefield. As noted previously, it is important to insure that the necessary trade-offs between firepower, mobility, and survivability provide the best tank for the future battlefield environment and that expenditures on tanks also provide equal or increased effectiveness over the same expenditures for other weapons systems. In other words, it is not only important that the MICV, for example, represent a quantum jump in the effectiveness over the M113 or Improved TOW vehicle, but that the funds expended on the MICV provide more force effectiveness than equal funds spent on improving other systems like the tank or artillery.

Generally, all actions on the battlefield are interactive. If, for example, one introduces the advanced attack helicopter into the force structure as a tank killer, then the value of our own tanks in the given force structure will be reduced because, as mentioned previously, a weapon system derives its value from the cumulative value of enemy weapons systems killed. Thus, if

Chart 17

COMCAP 77 BLUE DEFENSE

THEN HERE IS THE OUTCOME OF THE BATTLE
VALUE IS REMOVED FROM THE BATTLEFIELD AT A
RATE OF 0.16961 PER UNIT TIME
THE BLUE AND RED UEVs ARE 141.87 AND 179.72 RESECTIVELY
THE FORCE EFFECTIVENESS RATIO IS 0.7894

BLUE

SYSTEMS	WEV	x	NUMBER	=	SYSTEM VALUE		PERCENT OF BLUE FORCE STRENGTH DUE TO EACH WPN
A3**	1.00	x	47.0	=	47.00	A3**	33.128
A2**	0.91	x	24.0	=	21.84	A2**	15.314
TOW*	0.87	x	24.0	=	20.88	TOW*	14.636
DRA*	0.20	x	35.0	=	7.00	DRA*	5.007
INF*	0.00	x	421.0	=	0.00	INF*	1.103
AH**	1.48	x	4.0	=	5.92	AH**	4.169
81M*	0.00	x	12.0	=	0.00	81M**	0.019
4D**	0.09	x	10.0	=	0.90	4D**	0.653
155*	0.21	x	23.0	=	4.83	155*	3.393
8IN*	0.38	x	10.0	=	3.80	8IN*	2.671
175*	0.23	x	5.0	=	1.15	175*	0.794
CHA*	0.10	x	8.0	=	0.80	CHA*	0.545
HAW*	1.06	x	3.0	=	3.18	HAW*	2.249
F4**	2.32	x	6.0	=	13.92	F4**	9.822
F7**	2.30	x	4.0	=	9.20	F7**	6.497

UEV 141.87

RED

RED WEV VALUES AND NUMBER OF EACH SYSTEM

SYSTEMS	WEV	x	NUMBER	=	SYSTEM VALUE		PERCENT OF RED FORCE STRENGTH DUE TO EACH WPN
T62*	0.35	x	160.0	=	56.00	T62*	31.418
BR**	0.62	x	16.0	=	9.92	BR**	5.482
BM**	0.29	x	179.0	=	51.91	BM**	28.701
INF*	0.00	x	1435.0	=	0.00	INF*	0.008
SAG*	0.78	x	12.0	=	9.36	SAG*	5.193
73R*	0.10	x	12.0	=	1.20	73R*	0.661
AT**	0.42	x	8.0	=	3.36	AT**	1.862
120*	0.13	x	31.0	=	4.03	120*	2.265
122*	0.14	x	55.0	=	7.70	122*	4.352
152*	0.20	x	24.0	=	4.80	152*	2.690
MRL*	0.21	x	16.0	=	3.36	MRL*	1.881
130*	0.09	x	23.0	=	2.07	130*	1.185
Q23*	0.12	x	16.0	=	1.92	Q23*	1.086
SA6*	1.15	x	4.0	=	4.60	SA6*	2.554
TA**	1.60	x	12.0	=	19.20	TA**	10.663

UEV 179.72

Source: Office of Battlefield Systems Integration/MITRE, 1977

73

improved armor on a tank greatly reduces the lethality of enemy ATGMs, then the value of ATGMs to the enemy is greatly reduced and the value of our weapons that kill enemy ATGMS is also reduced. When the values of the ground-based Red tank killers (ATGM) are reduced, the value of the Red tactical air is appreciably increased because it becomes the major enemy tank killer. Concomitantly, the value of the Blue air defense, which counters the Red tactical air, becomes more important. Obviously, the increased armor protection for the XM-1 tank then under development was right on the money and consideration should be given to fielding an improved air defense gun along with the XM-1.

Thus it can be seen that all changes on the battlefield have a rippling effect. Each weapon system is linked to other weapon systems, both friendly and enemy, and all must be considered to understand the dynamics of the situation. Battlefield weapons systems involved in the central duel can for the sake of analysis and understanding be rolled up into eight categories: tank; anti-tank; mech infantry; dismounted infantry; attack helicopter; artillery; air defense; and tactical air. Each of these categories interacts in some way to each other. However, only certain linkages are major. These major interactions are what stress the weapons systems and must be thoroughly understood. Chart 18 illustrates a linkage diagram showing major interactions only. From such a diagram it is possible to isolate the linkage of given weapons systems to gain insights into interactions. Chart 19 has isolated Blue tanks in relation to the Red systems interacting with it. Perusal of this chart shows that when considering firepower, friendly tanks kill many enemy (note the arrowheads). Conversely, when considering survivability, many enemy weapons systems kill the friendly tanks (note the arrowheads). The numbers on the chart show that in the 1977 COMCAP simulation the friendly tanks contributed 48% of the value of the Blue force, whereas the Red weapons killing the Blue tank contributed 84% of the value of the Red force.

Now let's enter into the problem of design trade-offs for the Blue tanks. A pertinent question at the time was, what is more important, enhanced firepower or better survivability? Let us suppose that we want to increase our firepower. Depending upon how the firepower is improved, you could get varying effects. If the main gun were upgunned from 105mm to 120mm, then the major effect on the enemy would be to increase T62 kills, since with the same fire controls, a 105mm would obliterate the other weapon systems listed. Taking the survivability side of the coin, if new armor were placed on this tank it would affect almost all of the enemy weapon systems. Generally speaking, for those systems involved in the

Chart 18

INTERACTIVE WEAPONS SYSTEMS

LINKAGE DIAGRAM

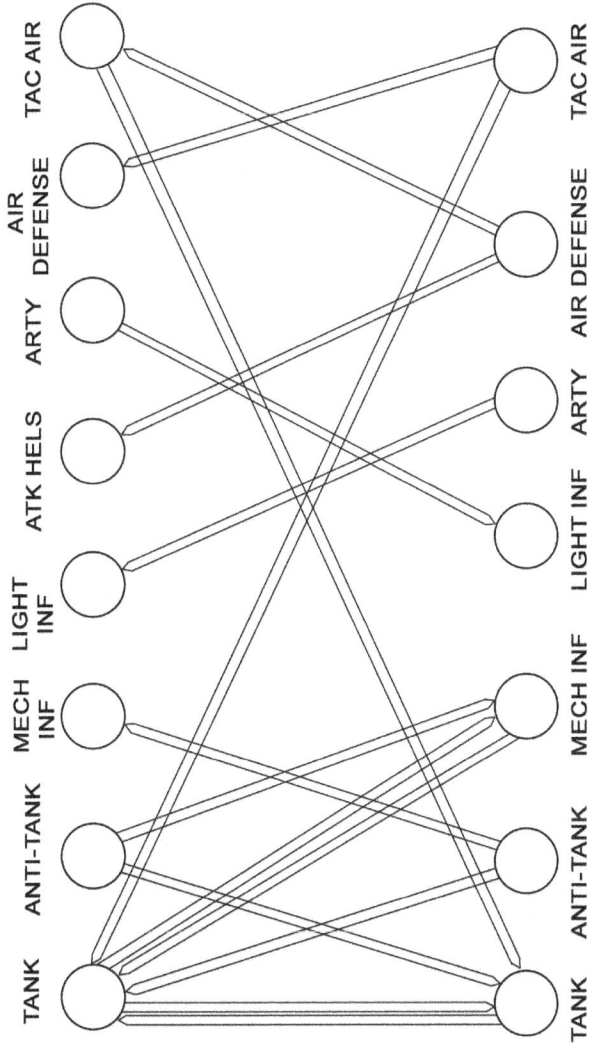

Source: Office of Battlefield Systems Integration, 1977

Chart 19

FORCE ON FORCE ANALYSIS

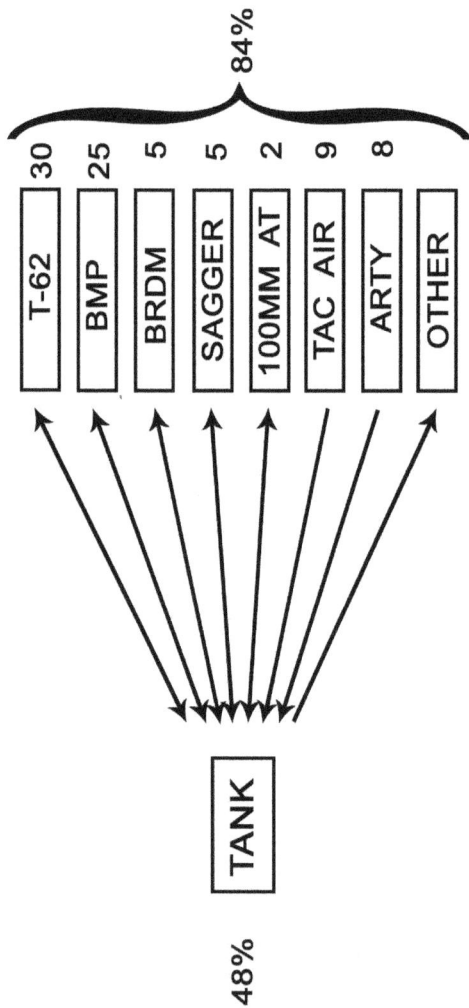

T-62	30
BMP	25
BRDM	5
SAGGER	5
100MM AT	2
TAC AIR	9
ARTY	8

84%

TANK

48%

FIREPOWER: ONE ON MANY
SURVIVABILITY: MANY ON ONE

OTHER

Source: Office of Battlefield Systems Integration, 1977

76

main battle where one system kills many and many kill it, improvements in survivability provide greater payoffs than equal improvements in firepower.

Let's not misunderstand what has been said. The end game is to kill the enemy. Therefore, firepower is the operative factor. But starting with the M60A3 tank and considering the overall battle, that is, the force effectiveness ratios, survivability has a greater payoff. In the example of survivability, the actual contribution of Blue tanks is reduced but the total force ratio increases. It is the combined arms team, the total force, that counts. Not the isolated individual weapon system, but the interactive total force system.

As stated previously, a central duel always takes place. This is the tank, anti-tank, mech infantry, and dismounted infantry combat. The stress of battle measured by attrition is in the central duel. In almost every case there is also a counterfire contribution to the central duel from artillery, tactical air, and attack helicopters, which can kill members of the central duel but are not in general killed by members of the central duel. Whenever counterfires are important you also find a counter-counterfire role played by air defense versus tactical air and helicopters and by artillery in a counterfire mode. In 1977, the counter-counterfire contributions to the main battle were small. They had to be improved through better fire control, target acquisition, and command and control.

The results of the central duel in the 1977 COMCAP war game are depicted in Chart 20. The numbers are the percentages of the unit effectiveness contributed by the eight functional groups of weapons systems involved in the central duel. You can see a general symmetry in that the total force contributions of both sides to the central duel are about the same, Blue 69% and Red 73%. However, one fact really stands out...the Blue infantry fighting vehicles (APCs) contribute little to the battle (however, the troops being carried and their ATGMs contribute when deployed). Compare this to the major contributions of the Red BMPs and BRDMs. The reason is obvious...the Blue APCs (IFVs) have little firepower. The critical requirement for a MICV becomes obvious. It was believed that a mech infantry vehicle with armament that can outgun the BMD was definitely one of the major requirements of the battlefield at the time.

Note also the contributions of the counterfire weapons, artillery, tactical air, and attack helicopters. The Red force in this game was not given attack helicopters. Counterfire weapons kill the systems involved in the central

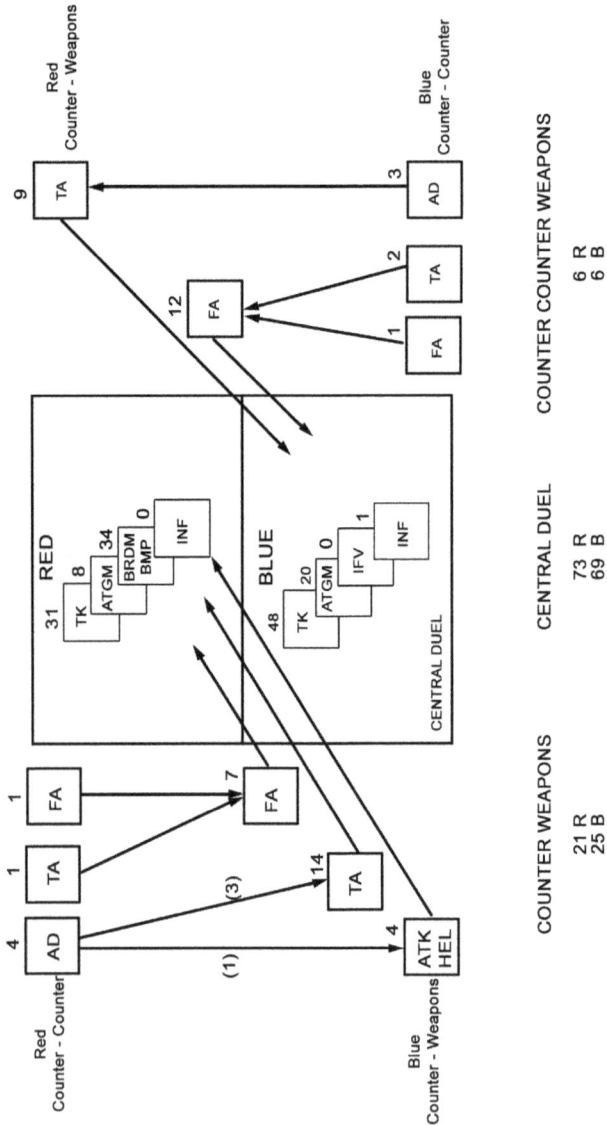

Chart 20
1977 FORCE ON FORCE
FER IS 0.79

Source: Office of Battlefield Systems Integration, 1977

duel. In fact, almost all of the 21% contribution of the Red counterfire weapons to the Red total force value is derived from killing Blue tanks.

In 1977, the counter-counterfire contributions of both Red and Blue to the main battle were small. In the future Blue's counterfire capabilities must be improved, not only to support the central duel but to be able to impede and attrit Red forces in Zone 2.

Blue artillery provides an insight into both counterfire and counter-counterfire activities. Blue artillery attrited many Red systems (one on many) and only the Red artillery and tactical air attrited the Blue artillery (few on one). Therefore, improvements in Blue firepower should be sought. Total Blue artillery force contributions were 6.9%, of which 5.6% was against Red armored vehicles, and 0.8% was against Red ATGMs, which together contributed 73% of the Red force strength. However, Blue contributions in counter-battery fire against Red artillery were an anemic 0.2%, primarily because Red artillery had greater range. Improved Conventional Munitions which would greatly improve fractional coverage would appreciably improve the Blue artillery kill rate against Red armored vehicles. Improved ranges would better the counter-battery situation as well as having a much greater impact when considering Zone 2 interdiction.

In our studies, we found no cases in which attack helicopters became as important as the tank or anti-tank systems unless the number of attack helicopters was increased to where they were more than half the number of tanks. The COMCAP force structure included four attack helicopters supporting a battalion sized unit and this in our opinion was about par for the situation. In that case, attack helicopters contributed only 4% of Blue force strength and their main contribution was killing T-62 tanks.

It is sobering to note that about 94% of the total force value of both sides was obtained by killing the participants of the central duel. As stated previously, 84% of Red force value was from killing Blue tanks. Once a MICV type vehicle is fielded, then the Reds will have to spread their lethality capability and tanks will not be nearly so stressed. This fact is very important. <u>To the extent we can improve our mech infantry, ATGMs and light infantry, we will have more effective tanks</u>. As it now stands, the US tank not only is the major contributor to the battle but it is by far the most stressed target. In this respect, we do not have a <u>balanced force</u>. While this situation obtains, survivability is the key to armored success. The XM1 is just the ticket for the modern battlefield. Its new armor and increased agility provide a quantum leap forward in survivability. At the same time, its enhanced fire control, enabling greater accuracy and a fire-on-the-move capability plus improved ammunition, adds to firepower.

Neither the US nor the Soviet armed forces were static. Both were developing new weapons systems and introducing them into their respective combat units. We set a time line for the introduction of a few new systems between 1975 and 1985, choosing what was considered some of the potential major improvements. Then, considering Blue defense and utilizing the COMCAP III base case we ran a continuous battlefield model as each system (Red and Blue) was introduced into the field. The purpose was to determine the force effectiveness ratios over time. Such an exercise was useful to obtain insights into gross weapons effectiveness but the exercise in and of itself definitely was <u>not rigorous</u> in methodology. A word of caution concerning the use of numbers in systems analysis is necessary. Numbers are generally never hard and often can be misleading. It is the trends and relative values that count. Individual numbers could be soft, but the trends and relative values were generally very consistent.

The FER for the central duel in 1985 will be discussed subsequently. However, the aforementioned exercise indicated that as new weapons were introduced the FERs are often appreciably affected. The order in which the systems were introduced and the resulting FERs are shown in Table 8.

Table 8
Continuous Introduction of New Weapons Systems

WEAPON	FER	
Base Case	.79	
Soviet Smoke	.73	
US ICM	.97	(Big improvement)
Soviet T-72 Tank	.97	
US XM-1 Tank	1.08	(Substantial improvement)
Soviet Tac Air	.99	(Substantial degradation)
US Improved AD	1.02	
Soviet ICM	.70	(Major degradation)
US EW	.75	
Soviet M 80	.69	
US AAH with Hellfire	.73	

In the aforementioned exercise major improvements in the FER were made by the introduction of improved conventional munitions (ICM). The ability of bomblets to seek armored vehicles over a large area is important to the central duel but also in attriting and slowing the Red reinforcements beyond the FEBA.

Note that the final FER after the new Blue and Red systems were introduced into the forces was not improved over the base case. The lesson learned by the exercise was simple...you cannot sit on your laurels but you must continuously seek to introduce combat effective systems or get left behind.

Note also that the suppressive effect of EW on Soviet communications and command systems had an improved outcome. EW will also have a major affect on Soviet follow-on echelons attempting to close the FEBA.

Up until now, the discussion has been on improvements in the WEV through increased survivability and firepower. Changes in the balance of systems and of course additional numbers of a given system will affect the FER. That is why reinforcing your own troops and slowing and attriting the enemy are so important. The following table shows how the addition of M60A-3 tanks affected the COMCAP 77 outcome.

Table 9
Improvements in the FER by Reinforcements

Number of M60-A-3		Force Effectiveness Ratio
Base Case	47	.79
	52	.81
	57	.83
	62	.85
	67	.87

The dynamic modeling methodology described is a valuable tool for estimating first order effects of potential battlefield changes. Once a costly war game scenario is available, it is quick and easy to apply in order to obtain the relative contributions of weapons systems. The major shortcoming of the method is that tactics, mobility and logistics are implicit, a function of the designers of the war games, and are therefore invariable.

The determination of weapons effectiveness by dynamic combat modeling is summarized in Chart 21. The central duel occurs in all battles and in it the Blue forces are supported by all the mission areas. The endgame is to defeat the Red forces, that is, to have a force effectiveness ratio greater than one. The key then is to have the maximum number of committed forces

Chart 21

WEAPON EFFECTIVENESS

COMBAT MODELING

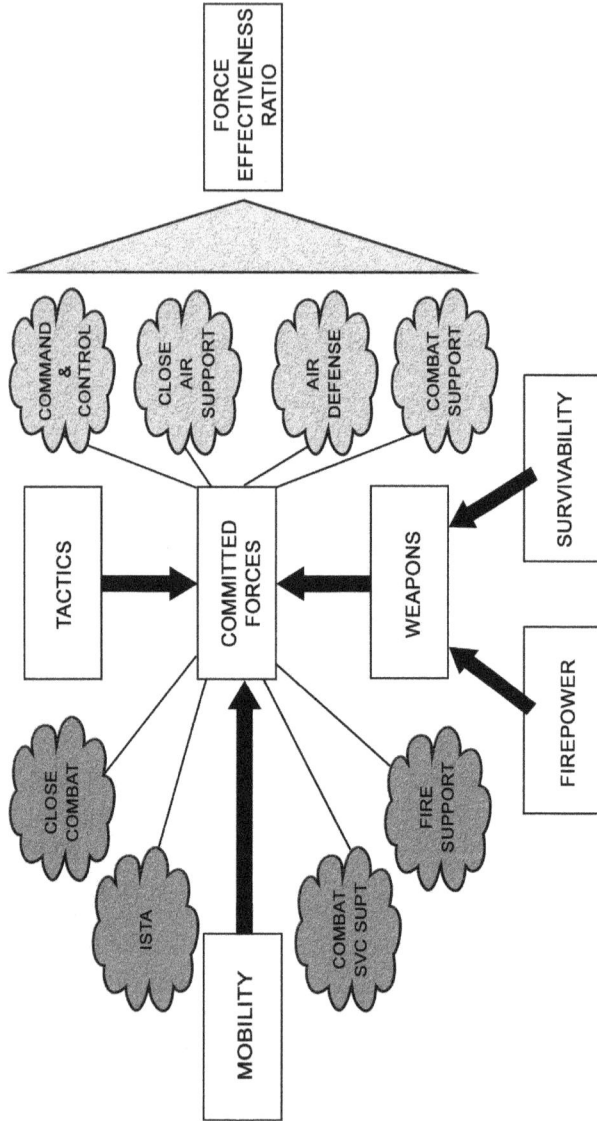

FORCE EFFECTIVENESS RATIO

COMMAND & CONTROL

CLOSE AIR SUPPORT

AIR DEFENSE

COMBAT SUPPORT

TACTICS

COMMITTED FORCES

WEAPONS

SURVIVABILITY

CLOSE COMBAT

ISTA

MOBILITY

COMBAT SVC SUPT

FIRE SUPPORT

FIREPOWER

Source: Office of Battlefield Systems Integration, 1976

outfitted with superior weapons at the critical area where success depends, among other factors, upon effective tactics at all echelons. Mobility is important to concentrate forces through reinforcements and weapons effectiveness is a function of firepower and survivability.

Looking to the future it was of interest to calculate the effects of which Red and Blue's ongoing system developments might have upon the 1985 central duel.

THE 1985 CENTRAL DUEL

Both the US and the Soviets intended to develop, produce, and field many new combat systems in the next decade. The US already had several promising major systems in development which would definitively improve close combat capabilities in the central duel (the XM-1 tank, the MICV armored personnel carrier, and the improved TOW vehicle as well as the advanced attack helicopter). With the exception of the helicopter, these were combat systems which the Soviets had already fielded and the US was just now playing catch-up. The Soviets were also upgrading their tanks to an all-new M-80 model. At this time the Soviets appeared to be mostly concentrating on improving their artillery and combat aviation capabilities. Utilizing the same gaming scenario as in COMCAP 77, we introduced the new equipment and ran COMCAP 85. The results are indicated in Chart 22 in the same format as for COMCAP 77. Notice for the Blue forces that the XM-1 has replaced the A-3 tank, the improved TOW vehicle replaces the TOW, the advanced attack helicopter replaces the AH, the DIVADS anti-aircraft gun replaces the Chapparal, and the MICV armored personnel carrier has been added. The Red force has replaced the M-72 tank with the M-80, they have self-propelled armored artillery, tactical air has improved capabilities, and they have added the attack helicopter.

A review of the schematic of the 1985 central duel at Chart 23 indicates several very important factors. First, the improvements in the Blue close combat systems have increased the force effectiveness ratio from 0.79 in 1977 to 0.90 in 1985. Secondly, with the addition of MICV infantry fighting vehicle (IFV) the Blue Close Combat forces are <u>much more balanced</u>. This has taken the pressure off the tanks. In 1977, 84% of the Red force strength was contributed by the Red weapons attriting the Blue tanks which made up 48% of the value of the Blue force, while in 1985 65% of the Red force's strength was contributed by weapons killing Blue tanks which made up 33% of the Blue force strength. The increased survivability of the XM-1 resulting from the improved armor and the

Chart 22

COMCAP 85 BLUE DEFENSE

THEN HERE IS THE OUTCOME OF THE BATTLE
VALUE IS REMOVED FROM THE BATTLEFIELD AT A
RATE OF 0.17348 PER UNIT TIME
THE BLUE AND RED UEVs ARE 198.06 AND 219.69 RESECTIVELY
THE FORCE EFFECTIVENESS RATIO IS 0.9015

BLUE

SYSTEMS	WEV	×	NUMBER	=	SYSTEM VALUE		PERCENT OF BLUE FORCE STRENGTH DUE TO EACH WPN
XM1*	1.00	×	47.0	=	47.00	XM1*	23.731
A2**	0.75	×	24.0	=	18.00	A2**	9.114
ITV*	0.81	×	24.0	=	19.44	ITV*	9.860
DRA*	0.17	×	35.0	=	5.95	DRA*	2.920
INF*	0.00	×	421.0	=	0.00	INF*	1.011
AAH*	2.56	×	4.0	=	10.24	AAH*	5.172
81M**	0.00	×	12.0	=	0.00	81M**	0.013
GS**	1.87	×	4.0	=	7.48	GS**	3.773
155*	0.37	×	28.0	=	10.36	155*	5.162
8IN*	0.48	×	10.0	=	4.80	8IN*	2.417
DIV*	0.55	×	8.0	=	4.40	DIV*	2.229
HAW*	3.59	×	3.0	=	10.77	HAW*	5.435
F4**	2.93	×	6.0	=	17.58	F4**	8.882
F7**	2.67	×	4.0	=	10.68	F7**	5.396
MCV*	1.09	×	27.0	=	29.43	MCV*	14.886
				UEV	198.06		

RED

RED WEV VALUES AND NUMBER OF EACH SYSTEM

SYSTEMS	WEV	×	NUMBER	=	SYSTEM VALUE		PERCENT OF RED FORCE STRENGTH DUE TO EACH WPN
M80*	0.33	×	160.0	=	58.50	M80*	26.625
BR**	0.30	×	16.0	=	4.84	BR**	2.204
BM**	0.27	×	179.0	=	48.16	BM**	21.922
INF*	0.00	×	1435.0	=	0.00	INF*	0.006
SAG*	0.61	×	12.0	=	7.39	SAG*	3.362
73R*	0.09	×	12.0	=	1.09	73R*	0.495
AT**	0.35	×	8.0	=	2.79	AT**	1.271
120*	0.19	×	31.0	=	5.75	120*	2.616
122*	0.23	×	55.0	=	12.77	122*	5.813
152*	0.35	×	24.0	=	8.32	152*	3.788
MRL*	0.37	×	16.0	=	5.96	MRL*	2.714
130*	0.14	×	23.0	=	3.31	130*	1.508
Q23*	0.23	×	16.0	=	3.71	Q23*	1.690
SA6*	3.51	×	4.0	=	14.02	SA6*	6.385
TA**	2.33	×	12.0	=	27.92	TA**	12.701
SAH*	1.89	×	8.0	=	15.16	SAH*	6.899
				UEV	219.69		

Source: Office of Battlefield Systems Integration/MITRE, 1977

Chart 23

1985 FORCE ON FORCE
FER IS 0.90

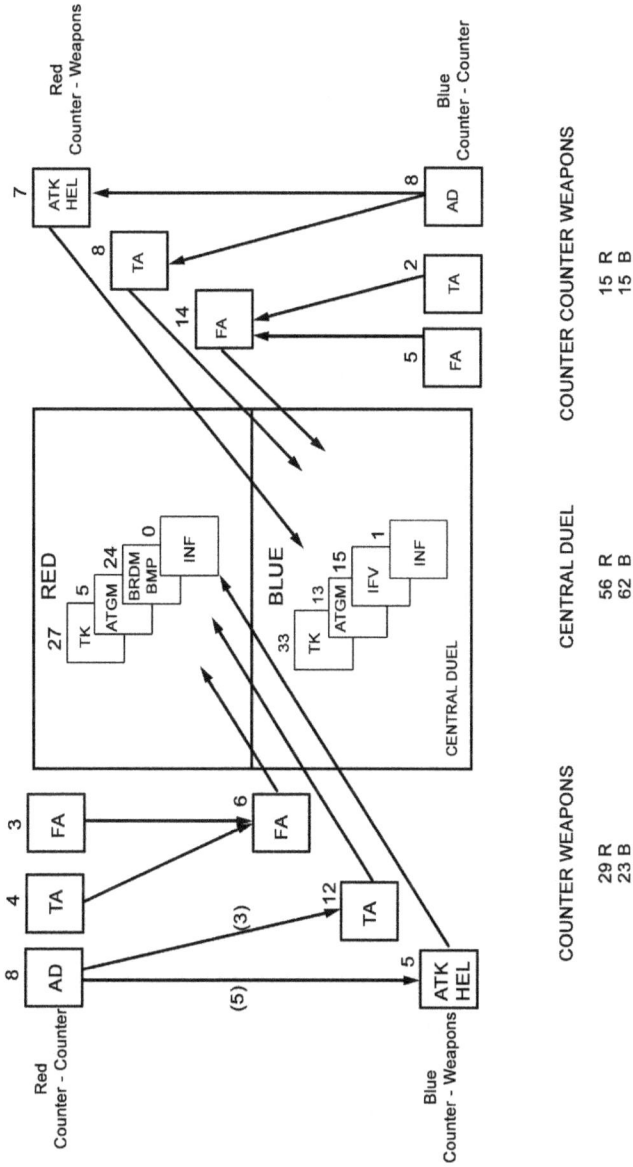

COUNTER WEAPONS	CENTRAL DUEL	COUNTER COUNTER WEAPONS
29 R 23 B	56 R 62 B	15 R 15 B

Source: Office of Battlefield Systems Integration, 1977

introduction of the MICV (now called the Bradley) has reduced the effectiveness of the Red Close Combat force. The Red force strength in the central duel has been reduced from 73% to 56%, with a concomitant increase in Red counter and counter-counter weapons from 27% to 44%. Seven percent of the increase resulted from the introduction of the Red attack helicopter.

The Soviets recognized they could effect a breakthrough and maintain the momentum in the attack only if they could effectively prevent NATO units from reinforcing the critical areas. For several years the Soviets had been concentrating on building up their counter and counter-counterfire weapons. They were modernizing TacAir at a great rate; they were out-producing the US in heavily armored attack helicopters; and they were improving and proliferating artillery, particularly self-propelled armored artillery. In other words, while we were necessarily concentrating on building up the weapons of the central duel the Soviets could afford to and were concentrating on counterweapons.

The air defense gun is the primary weapon with which to counter Soviet attack helicopters and tactical air in the forward battle area. Without an effective AD gun the Soviets would have a real edge in the near future. Because of the appreciable Soviet improvements in counterweapons, the contribution of the same numbers of Blue air defense guns to the future force structure will be almost three times as much in 1985 as it was in 1977, primarily from attriting the newly-introduced Red helicopter. When you compare the WEVs of Red tactical air and the Blue air defense systems in the 1977 COMCAP with the 1985 COMCAP results you find substantial improvements:

Table 10
Air Defense WEVs

	1977	1985
Red Tactical Air	1.60	2.33
Blue Hawk AD	1.06	3.59
Blue AD gun	0.10	0.55

There were major changes in the percent of Blue weapon force strength due to interactions with each Red weapon and vice versa in the COMCAP 1985 battle. It is interesting to note that 82% of Blue value came from killing Red armor (M80@40.30, BRDM @ 1.44, and BMP @ 40.19). Other major Blue values are from attriting Red air defense (6.02), attack helicopters (4.47), and tactical air (3.79). On the other hand, 80% of the

Red values were from killing blue armor (XM-I @ 48.16, M60A2 @ 17.85, and MICV @ 12.94). Other major Red values are from attriting Blue attack helicopter (5.24), artillery (4.72), and tactical air (2.83). The Blue values for attriting Red artillery were comparatively low at only 2.58 due to the fact that Red artillery was armored and, as mentioned previously, they still generally outgunned Blue artillery.

The effect of suppression upon the performance of individuals and weapons systems is an important element in the central duel. There are several potential sources of suppression: enemy fire, particularly artillery, enemy smoke, inclement weather and EW. Enemy artillery fires, for example, could cause the infantrymen to take cover thereby rendering the ATGM ineffective for the period they were under fire. Several simulations in COMCAP 77 were run considering smoke and inclement weather. In both cases large area obfuscation favored the force with the most combatants since it reduced the effectiveness of direct fire weapons. In the smoke cases we considered that both the blue and Red direct fire would be reduced 50% and the Blue indirect fire reduced 25%. There was no change in Red indirect fire. The effect was to increase the value of artillery and tactical air and therefore air defense. The base case force ratio was somewhat reduced. Severe ground fog and non-flying weather, which was typical of the area in Central Europe, caused an even greater reduction in the force ratio because it affected all weapons systems. Since limited visibility situations benefitted the enemy, Blue must develop a millimeter radar or equivalent device that will penetrate smoke and fog[1].

As quoted previously, Soviet doctrine called for the major utilization of smoke as an important countermeasure to "ensure the screening of troops...and produce disturbances in the work of gun laying systems."

As the Soviets said, smoke will obfuscate visual sightings, neutralize current new IR devices and degrade laser weapons. Therefore we must accelerate see through capabilities (FLIR), develop millimeter wave length trackers, improve land navigation (gyro-compass), and improve our own smoke capabilities.

The emphasis of the aforementioned has been upon assessing the relative combat capabilities of weapons systems in a threat scenario for which outputs were developed. The primary weapons characteristics of engaged combat force are firepower and survivability. The dynamic model allowed major effects of changes in weapons firepower, survivability, and weapons mixes to be easily determined and the process was applied to a great number of variations.

Dynamic force modeling of the central duel indicated several developmental areas of great promise, a few of which, happily, were ongoing:

1)	Tank survivability (ongoing)
2)	Need for an infantry fighting vehicle (ongoing)
3)	Requirement for improved ICMs and ARMs (ongoing)
4)	Requirement to see through smoke and fog (needs R&D)
5)	Requirement for improved AD gun (R&D)
6)	Need for improved ATGMs (R&D)
7)	Requirement for millimeter radar (R&D)

Looking out to 1985 when the ongoing developmental systems would be fielded, there was a marked improvement in the FER, from .79 to .90. This still was not sufficient to turn the tide of battle. An important element to assure victory was the necessity for Blue to reinforce the central duel. However, Red had been developing counter weapons that could have a serious effect on Blue's capability to reinforce the main battle area. Consequently, it was important to study the capabilities of both sides to reinforce the battlefield.

Recall that Soviet doctrine called for the massing of large armored force in depth in order to concentrate the attack and to effect a breakthrough. Thus, to maintain a suitable force ratio at the decisive engagement Blue must attrit the engaged Red force (central duel), slow and attrit Red reinforcements (Zone 2), and reinforce the battle area.

It was our opinion at the time that the Soviets recognized they could effect a breakthrough and maintain the momentum in the attack only if they could effectively prevent NATO units from reinforcing the critical area. The following schematic taken from a Soviet publication indicates their intention of interdicting Blue rear echelons (Chart 24). The Soviet build-up of tactical air and attack helicopters was not only to attack blue forces at the main battle area but also to interdict enemy forces in the rear to prevent reinforcements. The major increase in the lethality of the Red counter-counter weapons (from 6 to 15 percent of the total force) could seriously impede Blue's capability to reinforce the central duel. Consequently it was important to study the interdiction of the echeloned in depth Red forces, which we believed to be Red's major vulnerability, as well as considering

Chart 24

SOVIET INTERDICTION CONCEPT

INFLICTING DAMAGE ON THE ENEMY BY FIRE DURING THE MEETING ENGAGEMENT
(ON THE FURTHER APPROACHES AND DURING HIS DEPLOYMENT)

Source: Tanks and Tank Troops Mil Pub House Marshal of Tank Troops A. K. Babadzhan Yan. ED.

means to improve Blue's ability to reinforce, thus increasing the force effectiveness ratio through force multiplication.

The previous dynamic analyses of the central duel took into consideration the effects of changes in firepower, survivability, weapon mixes, and suppression upon weapons systems. Mobility is a very important capability of weapons systems and the mobility capabilities of armored vehicles were built into the scenarios of the central duel. When considering reinforcements to the main battle area, mobility or the lack thereof assumes prime importance as both forces attempt to interdict each other.

BATTLEFIELD INTERDICTION

In the previous discussion of the threat it was seen that Soviet dispositions at the time of initial contact for a classic breakthrough of two tank divisions or for a meeting engagement of one tank division were spread in depth from 80 to 100 kilometers and it could take up to 20 hours for the second echelon troops to close on the FEBA. Therefore, it was abundantly clear that the US must have the capability to rapidly attrit and slow the large number of Soviet vehicles and weapons at great distances from the FEBA. This is a very different scenario than the central duel. The ability to kill and slow the enemy is primarily a function of long range weapons and tactical air and the ability of ISTA systems to detect, locate, and identify targets in real time through a distributed information system.

Improvements expected in target acquisition, conventional munitions, and precision guided missiles indicated that attack on enemy targets well behind the FEBA could have a significant affect in the future on the outcome of battle. We have previously noted that Soviet doctrine calls for maintaining momentum, requiring that their echeloned reinforcements close rapidly to the main battle area. This is probably Red's primary vulnerability. We must delay and attrit the enemy at the FEBA and his reinforcements while concurrently reinforcing our own troops at the critical battle area.

MITRE investigated[2] the effect of attriting and slowing down the Red attack by giving the Blue force a battlefield interdiction capability to counter the numerical superiority of the attacking Red force. They conducted many analyses and the basic study will be discussed to illustrate several factors of the interdiction situation. Tactical air was not included in this case, a situation which would occur during inclement weather. Assuredly, tactical air is absolutely vital for Zone 2 interdiction. The model was structured simply with two types of forces; short range (tanks) and long range (artillery). Blue forces engaged the enemy at the FEBA with short range forces able to kill only Red short range forces and long range artillery able to kill either type of enemy systems. Blue concentrated all forces at the FEBA in a static defense while Red attacked in three waves moving through Zone 2 to the FEBA. Blue was assumed to have a good target acquisition capability and some type of weapons guidance enabling it to attack individual Red targets, reasonable assumptions for future interdictive warfare, but which were not then available.

The Red force attacked with three echelons of 1500, 1000, and 1000 tanks and with 1000 artillery pieces in the first echelon. The defending Blue force was given 1000 tanks and 500 artillery pieces. Blue, because of its defensive

posture and superior weaponry, had a 5:1 superiority in kill rate per
weapon. Tactical assumptions were that each side allocated 20% of its
artillery to counter the enemy artillery, and Blue allocated the remaining
80% of its long range weapons to interdiction. If more than one Red wave
was in Zone 2 at any time, Blue interdicted only the last wave to enter Zone
2. The Red echelons entered Zone 2 at six and twelve hours respectively.
The Zone 2 rear boundary was 30 km. beyond the FEBA and the
unimpeded Red rate of advance was 10 km/hr.

When Blue interdicted the Red forces, Blue won the battle with 264 tanks
remaining. The tank exchange ratio was 4.45. Interestingly, the Blue
interdictive fires slowed the Red echelons down to 8 km/hr in the first
wave and to about 5.2 km/hr in the follow-on echelons.

The effects of interdiction resulted from two factors: the attrition of the
Red initial echelon before reaching the FEBA where the tanks became
engaged and the slowing of successive Red echelons which prevented a
build-up at the main battle area. The relative importance of these two
factors was determined by running an intermediate case where there was no
slowing up of Red movement. Red won that battle with 379 tanks left and
the tank exchange ratio was 3.10. Interestingly, 75% of the base case
success resulted from slowing down the succeeding Red wave.

The influence of interdictive fires was measured by running the model
without any Blue attacks in Zone 2. In that variant, Blue artillery was
allocated 80% to Red tanks and 20% to Red artillery. Without interdiction
Red won with 853 tanks left and the exchange ratio was reduced to 2.65.
This iteration may be closer to actual combat because it is unlikely that a
commander would allocate significant amounts of artillery away from the
troops in contact to interdict enemy forces in Zone 2, particularly under
non-flyable weather conditions.

The attrition rates utilized in the model were rather high. Blue tanks killed
Red tanks at the rate of .2 kills per hour in the scenario of a 12-hour
combat day. If the intensity of combat was reduced, then the battle would
have lasted much longer, requiring the Red velocity of advance to be greatly
reduced, making the model very sensitive to the number and kill rates of
Blue artillery. Since Blue relatively did not have a large quantity of artillery,
the kill rate was of paramount importance. We gave Blue artillery dual
purpose ICMs, precision guided munitions, and capable ISTA systems,
including RPVs, systems that were not yet available.
Our base model investigated the effects of various capabilities and strategies
for battlefield interdiction in Zone 2A on battle outcomes. However, it was

only one of many available models and strategies and the findings were not rigorous. Nevertheless, it provided several important results. First, killing Red reinforcements is very difficult and consequently second echelon attrition effects were not that great. Actually, present Blue artillery capabilities are definitely inadequate. Secondly, the effects of delaying Red reinforcements are potentially very significant. Thirdly, tactical air is absolutely essential to the successful interdiction of Red forces.

In Central Europe, there are many days when the weather precludes tactical air support. That was the aforementioned base case. We ran many other cases with tactical air, varying both artillery and tactical air allocations between close combat support and interdiction efforts. In all cases with tactical air the slowing of the rate of Red's second echelon advance was much more important than second echelon attrition. The ability to concentrate tactical air made it more effective than artillery. Scatterahle mines were also very effective in slowing the Red rate of advance.

In order to move through Zone 2 and reinforce the central duel at a high velocity, Red forces would have to move on roads where they would be highly vulnerable to detection and attack. Once the Red formations were detected it was presumed that the tracked vehicles would move overland but the large number of wheeled vehicles would continue to be road bound. Interdiction attacks would cause Red to adopt movement tactics which are much slower but which would ensure a higher Red survivability. Blue interdiction by slowing the Red rate of advance ensured the maintenance of a suitable force ratio at the central duel enabling Blue to attrit the Red engaged forces. Interdiction definitely is an important factor in determining the outcome of combat.

The Soviets were well aware of the importance of the second echelon attack. A.A. Sidorenko, Director of Military Science states[3]:

> "Second echelons were the basic means of exploiting success and conducting an attack at high rates and to a great depth. Where they were weak or were not committed in time, the attack developed not only slowly, but even died down."

Chart 25 is a schematic of a meeting engagement and depicts the three actions necessary to maintain a suitable force ratio. At the moment of contact the initial force ratio is probably about two. The enemy intends to reinforce the battle with second echelon troops to obtain and overwhelming force ratio of at least six. <u>Attrition</u> commences immediately and the interdiction of enemy troops in Zone 2 <u>slows</u> his rate of advance. However, it is by means of <u>friendly reinforcements</u> that the defensive force ratio is kept at a suitable level thus assuring victory.

All three actions are generally necessary to maintain a suitable defensive force ratio of 3:1.

Several aspects of mobility, which would enable Blue to reinforce the central duel, have been mentioned tangentially. One was the importance of highly mobile and protected armored vehicles not vulnerable to enemy artillery suppression and capable of all-terrain movement. Another was excellent air defense weapons including acquisition capabilities to defeat enemy air, and of course, the ability to determine the location of the enemy's main attack.

Success in having effective force multiplication was a function of the effectiveness of direct and indirect fire weapons systems which depended upon target acquisition systems that detected and located enemy targets and reported the information in real time to control centers which then could maneuver units and determine whether to fire or not and if to fire assigned the responsibility to a given force unit. In other words, ISTA and C&C were the keys to success and in 1976 these mission areas were far from optimized, and that's putting it mildly, as will be explained subsequently.

Chart 25

MAINTAINING SUITABLE FORCE RATIOS

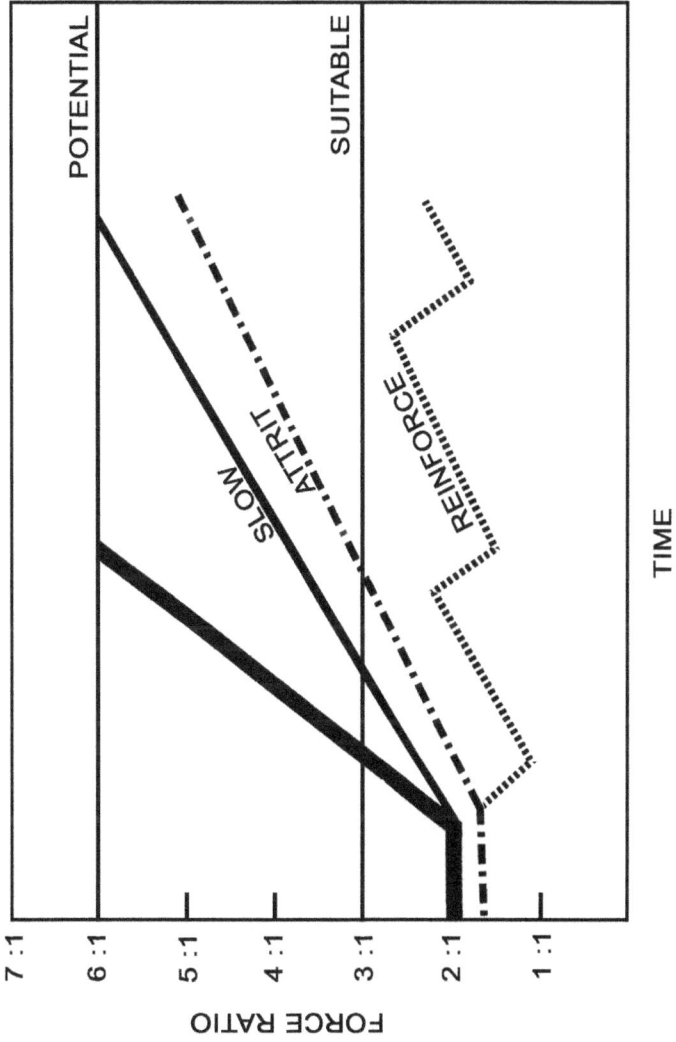

POTENTIAL

SUITABLE

SLOW

ATTRIT

REINFORCE

FORCE RATIO

7 :1
6 :1
5 :1
4 :1
3 :1
2 :1
1 :1

TIME

Source: Office of Battlefield Systems Integration, 1976

FORCE MULTIPLICATION

Summarizing the aforementioned, considering in 1976 that the forces of the Soviet Union were the current major threat, we should have been acquiring those equipment items that would provide the Army its greatest combat power relative to the Soviet Union. **Combat Power** is defined as the aggregate weapons lethality of engaged forces (units, soldiers, cross-hairs) as bounded by the situation (type of combat, terrain, season, weather, etc.). For a given situation (e.g., Europe, winter, Fulda Gap, Soviet surprise attack) our Combat Power is then a function of <u>weapons lethality/survivability</u> and the number of <u>engaged combatants</u>. We can increase our Combat Power through **Force Multipliers and Weapons Enhancements** where these terms are defined as follows:

> Force Multiplier is the friendly increase or enemy decrease of engaged cross hairs.
> Weapons Enhancement is the friendly increase or enemy decrease of weapons lethality.

Although combat power is important, the bottom line is relative combat power, i.e., for the given situation, will we be victorious?

The aforementioned <u>highly simplified aspects</u> of an infinitely complex situation are summarized in <u>gross terms</u> below[1]:

$$\text{Equation 2: Relative Combat Power} = \frac{Pb}{Pr} = S \frac{Fb}{Fr} \left(\frac{lb}{lr} \right)^{n}$$

Where: S is a situation dependent factor

Fb

Fr is the relative force of engaged troops (units, soldiers, cross-hairs).

lb

lr is the relative lethality of equivalently sized tactical units.

n is a Lanchestian derived constant, always less than 1.

Looking to real life, given a Soviet attack on V Corps defending the Fulda Gap the situation factor (S) is usually "guesstimated" at 3, i.e., defense over offense. The Warsaw Pact has an overall superiority in numbers of 3:1 in Central Europe so we must presume they will at least double their combatants at the critical point, i.e., a force ratio of 6:1.

Considering weapons enhancements, the COMCAP models determined the force effectiveness ratio of the central duel which was the aggregate effect of the combatants weapons lethalities, which were:

  1977   FER = .7894
  1985   FER = .9015

AMSAA and BSI conducted separate studies to determine the US/Soviet ratio of weapons lethality in the central duel for those years. The lethality ratio at five different ranges from the FEBA out to 2500 meters in 500 meter increments were determined and an average lethality ratio was calculated. With all the great improvements in US weapons (M-1 tank, Bradley fighting vehicle, Divads AD gun, improved TOW vehicle, etc.) the weapons lethality ratio improved from about 1.7 in 1977 to 2.0 in 1985, i.e., 17.6%.

Interestingly, the AMSAA lethality ratios when used in the combat power equations with the COMCAP 1977 and 1985 values gave identical Lanchestian exponential constants of 0.86.

Considering only weapons enhancements in Equation 2, that is holding the force ratio constant, the improvement in Blue weapons lethality from 1977 to 1985 increased the relative combat power by 14.2%, from .7894 to .9015.

When Blue forces are outnumbered and subject to surprise attacks they must fight with the weapons on hand when Red attacks. Therefore, weapons enhancements are very important, yet the FER of .9015 indicates that Red wins.

Consequently, to win, Blue must rely on Force Multiplication. There are three levels of force multiplication:

Tactical	Concentrate engagement of theater forces at critical battle area and attrit and impede enemy reinforcements.
Strategic	Reinforce with reserve troops not in theater.
Structural	For a given size organization to increase number of combat weapons.

The highly simplified aforementioned formula applies to tactical force multiplication. The 1977 and 1985 COMCAP dynamic modeling was predicated on an initial Soviet 3:1 advantage of engaged fires in the central duel. Recall that motorized and armored follow-up divisions were stretched some 60 to 100 kilometers behind the FEBA when the "balloon went up." When these second echelon troops closed on the central duel then the enemy could have a 6:1 force advantage. Equation 1, page 65 indicated that the ultimate force advantage in the central duel depended upon friendly and enemy reinforcements and attrition.

Holding all factors in the equations the same except the relative force ratios, then the following cases apply. If through effective ISTA and C&C the Blue command was able to discern the location of the Red main attack and was able by mobility to reinforce the central duel with 20% additional forces (from Fb to 1.2 Fb) then the relative combat power in 1985 would have increased from .9015 to 1.082, foretelling a positive outcome.

On the other hand, if Blue did not reinforce and the Red second echelon, as the result of excellent Blue ISTA and effective fires by artillery and TACAIR attacking the Red reinforcements and those units in bivouac and assembly areas were attrited and slowed so that the total engaged Red force was reduced by 20% (from 6 Fr to 4.8 Fr) then the relative combat power in 1985 would have increased 25% from .9015 to 1.127.

More importantly, if Blue reinforced by 20% and if 20% of the Red forces were prevented from joining the battle, then the relative combat power in 1985 would have increased from .9015 to 1.352, an increase of 50%, insuring a definite blue victory.

These highly simplified, very rough back of the envelope type calculations illustrate the importance of force multiplication. <u>Force multipliers are powerful!</u>

Important factors in tactical force multiplication are the ISTA and Command and Control mission areas in order to identify the location of the main enemy attack and to acquire enemy targets in Zone 2. However, previous cost analysis indicated that these two mission areas were probably under-funded. A review of the DCSOPS Army "Top 40" R&D and Procurement Lists published 9 March 1976 conclusively indicated that the Army's efforts were mostly directed toward increasing combat lethality[2]. Of the 40 systems, 24 were for improved lethality/survivability with 71% of the funding whereas only 8 systems with 16% of the funding were for force multiplication efforts only. Increasing combat lethality is a back-breaking route to travel; first, because we are always pushing the state of the art; and, second, because our hard-earned advantages are compounded less than linearly. Nevertheless, this is an essential route to take.

The technology exists to concentrate our forces and to disperse the enemy rear echelons while attriting his engaged forces. We must prioritize ISTA and Command and Control in order to maximize combat development and make major improvements in relative combat power for the best financial outlay. Both ISTA and command and control systems required much more attention.

Strategic force multipliers are generally bounded by the ability of the Air Force and Navy to provide the means (e.g., C-5 aircraft or Navy ships) necessary to transport men and equipment to the Theater of Operations. Strategic intelligence gathering is of great importance in determining the probable time and place of an enemy attack.

Structural force multipliers are also very important and in the past have been relatively ignored. Once a TO&E for a unit has been determined it is generally inflexible. The Army should be vigorously attempting to refine unit structures as new weapons are available and as field training exercises and battle simulation studies indicate potential areas of improvement. For example, our studies showed in 1977 that a more balanced cost effective force which would take the stress off the tank and increase combat power required more TOWs. Flexibility to change the combat force structure to fit the enemy situations, terrain and weather is vitally needed. The Army must maximize its combat power with the forces and weapons available and this is a continuing iterative process.

As an example, in Vietnam in 1968 our division was located in the inundated Delta. Initially, the division had eight straight-legged infantry battalions and two mechanized battalions. The mech battalions, particularly during the rainy season, could not operate effectively in the inundated Delta terrain. We wanted to exchange a mech battalion for a straight-legged battalion. It was made possibly only by the personal negotiations of two division commanders to effect such an exchange of battalions.

At the time (1976), the Army was definitely moving in the right direction with its Division Restructuring Study. The Army recognized that at great cost it was procuring a new family of armored weapons systems which could greatly improve combat effectiveness. It decided to integrate and optimize the new weapons systems within the tactical concepts for modern warfare to maximize firepower forward at the right place at the right time. The concept was to restructure to smaller maneuver companies and battalions with more battalion-sized organizations allowing units to move quickly and reposition faster. Combined arms were to be integrated and combat actions coordinated at battalion level. The study concluded that current organizations were not weapons systems oriented. A TOW company separate from the rifle companies was recommended. The full potential of combat power was to be generated by rapidly integrating combined arms relying heavily on well executed intelligence guided operations to obtain "combat multipliers." That was right on! Units should be able to adapt weapons and personnel to the potential combat situation.

NATO success in Europe in countering a potential Soviet attack would require the deployment of forces well forward and in depth throughout the defensive sector in order to continuously attrit the enemy from successive terrain oriented prepared positions while slowing the attack by suppressive means, i.e., artillery fires, obstacles, mine field barriers, EW, and smoke. The key to success would be to be to concentrate combat power at the decisive place and time thus obtaining a force ratio advantage. This would require excellent ISTA and Command and Control mission area capabilities, which unfortunately, at the time, were not anywhere near optimum. These two mission areas as well as the close combat mission area are briefly discussed subsequently.

MISSION AREA ANALYSES

All nine mission areas were analyzed in depth, each of which contributed importantly to the Army's overall combat capabilities. However, for the purposes of this book only the major aspects of the three key mission areas of Close Combat, ISTA, and Command Systems will be reviewed.

CLOSE COMBAT MISSION AREA

The critical battle occurs at the FEBA, the central duel, and all mission areas are involved, primarily the close combat mission area, which includes five functional groups of systems: tank, mechanized infantry, anti-tank, combat aviation, and light weapons (infantry). When considering weapon effectiveness it is instructive to focus initially on the tank, which is the most important contributor to the central duel where the battle outcome determines victory or defeat.

The Tank

The tank was born amidst the stalemate of World War I to restore mobility to the battlefield which was then dominated by the firepower of the machine gun and artillery. The British application of massed tanks to conduct offensive operations at the Battle of Cambrai in November 1917 contributed to a decisive victory, and the "Age of Armor" was launched. Now, over fifty years later, the tremendous losses of armor by both sides in the Yom Kippur War, perceived by many to be the result of anti-tank guided missiles (ATGM), has been heralded by many as the death knell for the Age of Armor. An important question then is, "What is the status of the tank?"

Notwithstanding the late successes of the tank in World War I, military authorities between the great wars could not agree on the tank's tactical role, its optimum characteristics, or even its potential as a decisive weapon. That all changed when the German Blitzkrieg tactics forged military thinking into a consensus that the tank was the primary offensive weapon on the battlefield and that the number one requirement for tanks was to kill other tanks. These two ideas dominated the design of tanks for the next thirty years.

Each of the major combatants ended World War II with a tank which, in varying degrees, met the perceived requirements for a lethal, well-protected, highly mobile main battle tank which could be used in massed assaults or as part of combined operations and was effective in tank-on-tank engagements. The final configuration of a tank is often the result of the interaction of many broad factors, including national policy, the economic situation, perceived threats, and military tactics. Synthesis is difficult, even at the tanker level, where he is confronted with conflicting requirements between firepower, mobility, and survivability. Ultimately, the user is required to accept a pragmatic but rarely satisfactory balance amongst the three major design characteristics. In other words, tank design is a series of trade-offs.

Although at times one design characteristic has been emphasized at the expense of another, for example, firepower over mobility, the driving factor involved in the trade-offs has been the perceived use (doctrine) of the tank. In order to fully understand the evolution of tanks, we believe it is essential to review the three major combat capabilities of a weapons system; that is, firepower, mobility, and survivability (protection). The tank is unique among land combat systems in that it is the only weapon that successfully incorporates these essential capabilities to a high degree.

Firepower

The value of a weapons system is measured by the cumulative value of enemy weapons which it kills. Consequently, firepower is the end game. The basic requirement is to destroy opposing armor and other more vulnerable targets. This necessitates the ability to acquire and hit enemy targets at the greatest practical range, considering the spectrum of climatic and visibility conditions. These aspects of firepower can generally be realized as the result of the size of the main gun, the main gun muzzle velocity, and the sophistication of fire control. The integration is measured on the battlefield by the probabilities of hit and kill. Since defeating enemy tanks has been the driving force in tank design, gun development has been in a see-saw competition with the increased thickness of armor. As armor protection increased, the need for projectiles to deliver more energy on the target was manifested. Since kinetic energy is a function of mass and velocity, there has been an almost continuous upgrading of the main gun caliber, thereby insuring greater projectile mass, as well as increased velocity. This trend toward larger projectiles has meant a concomitant reduction in stowed rounds. Lately, there have been major improvements in projectile penetration mechanics through the adoption of more exotic materials, such as tungsten and depleted uranium, for the penetrators.

There has been a steady increase in bore diameter and velocity. Although the development of fire control systems has been less obvious in that different combinations of components resulting in varying degrees of sophistication have occurred, the trend has been definitely towards increased sophistication. This includes improved stabilization; enhanced range determination, utilizing such state-of-the-art devices as laser range finders and solid state components; stabilized sight/gun systems; magnified sights; and night vision equipment, to include image intensification and thermal imaging. Although the Soviets have lagged behind in the sophistication of their fire control, they have had larger guns with higher muzzle velocities, and the net effect, when considering hit probability, is currently a standoff.

Mobility

Mobility also includes many components, such as the engine, transmission, and suspension, and capabilities, such as the ability to negotiate obstacles, ground pressure, cruising range, and transportability. The weight of a tank, which is a function primarily of protection, influences all of the mobility factors. The trends in protection and thus weight have been ever upward. This means that power packs, in order to provide more horsepower per ton, have had to grow more dramatically. One of the areas of recent major breakthroughs in the 1970s has been the US and German development of 1500 horsepower diesel and turbine engines. The cruising range of tanks, which affects their endurance and logistical requirements, has also been improved. Cruising range is primarily a function of weight, engine efficiency, fuel capacity and, naturally, the terrain. Transportability is usually defined as the ability to deliver the tank to its operational area via exogenous prime movers, such as rail, motor transport, and air. Transportability has done much to insure that the weight, height, and width of tanks stay within fairly well-defined norms. Although the US M60 series of tanks was an excursion from the heights of other world tanks, the advent of the XM1 will see a return to a lower profile, which in turn will beneficially influence survivability.

Survivability

The most unique feature of tanks is their armor. Tanks were initially developed to overcome the World War I imbalance between firepower and mobility by providing protection. However, armor protection is not the only aspect of survivability. Other important factors include the ability to avoid detection and acquisition, utilizing low silhouettes and on-board smoke, as well as design features which insure that if a tank is hit it is not destroyed, such as compartmentalization, and lately, the very important factor of agility which measures a tank's capability to accelerate and decelerate to avoid being hit by ATGMs. In fact, ATGMs in recent years have had more influence on survivability than enemy tank guns. This is the first breakthrough in the long tradition of primarily designing tank vs tank. The ATGM has also provided a dilemma for designers of armor protection in that armor which defeats chemical energy rounds is not optimized to defeat kinetic energy rounds.

From the aforementioned discussion of major weapons characteristics, it is obvious that a tank's ultimate configuration is an expression of the interaction of many varying interests requiring a large number of trade-offs. The importance of the trade-offs to the overall operational capability has been mainly a judgmental factor. Several interesting and excellent studies have recently been done in order to measure the worth of US tanks, one conducted by the Concepts Analysis Agency, and the other by the Tank Special Study Group. Both of these used as their basis the firepower, survivability, and mobility characteristics. Utilizing the Delphi approach, the studies weighed a large number of variables to measure the worth of a tank. When the combined results of the studies, normalized as effectiveness indices utilizing the M60A1 as standard, are plotted on Chart 16 the continuing growth of the worth of US tanks from World War II to date is portrayed. If dynamic modeling had been used then the important improvements of the XM1, particularly survivability, would have extended its effectiveness index completely off the scale of the chart. It is one of the failures of linear measures that they cannot take into consideration the dynamics of warfare.

All countries have pretty much settled on a single main battle tank whose general design characteristics have converged to the point where tanks are more alike than different. Yet there are differences. The Soviets have designed their tank primarily for an offensive role on the European continent, where they consider that their massive numbers will overwhelm and crush the enemy. Consequently, the Soviets have not designed for crew comfort because there will always be a fresh crew available. They do not have sophisticated fire control because they plan to close rapidly to within close range under the cover of heavy artillery fire and smoke. They have not increased the size of their tanks to carry a larger basic load because they do not wish to pay the penalties associated with the decision. In short, the Soviet Union is prepared to accept fairly heavy tank losses while the US is not. Tank design similarities are fostered by the almost universally accepted prioritization of tank versus tank. The internal tank community's insistence upon the "one-on-one" syndrome, that is, analyses comparing one's new tanks with one's previous models and the current enemy models, has resulted in a continuing evolutionary growth in capabilities that cannot fully evaluate the dynamic realities of warfare as they will exist in the future.

Anti-Tank Guided Missiles

Up to now, I have not discussed whether ATGMs have in fact sounded the death knell to the "Age of Armor." Nothing did more to shift the Army's focus from the conflict in Southeast Asia to the threat in Central Europe than the Yom Kippur War of 1973. The intensity of the battle measured in terms of armored vehicles lost was astonishing in that tank losses, for example, were greater than the totality of US tanks stationed in Central Europe. Seventy-five percent of the committed tanks were lost in the first eighteen hours of combat[1]. Analysis of the Yom Kippur War was still ongoing in 1976, as all sides strove to take full advantage of the "lessons learned."[2] Soviet Marshall A. A. Grechko's views on this war, quoted here, appeared to have great validity[3]:

> "At the present time the struggle between armor and anti-tank skills has been transferred to the scientific laboratory, to the proving ground and to industrial production. Receiving an answer to the question, 'who dominates whom' demands the solution of numerous complicated problems."

There are many aspects of "who dominates whom?" including tactics, doctrine, organization, force mixes, training, product improvement, and developmental opportunities. Each of these approaches to fixing the problems varies in cost and time. To facilitate analyses we divided anti-armor systems into four components: acquisition means, platforms, guidance, and the munitions.

Acquisition Means: Anti-armor acquisition can be very simple, such as using the naked eye, or very complex, particularly beyond the line of sight, where enemy armored vehicles might be acquired by a standoff target acquisition system (SOTAS) using moving target indicator (MTI) radar and identified by means of remotely piloted vehicles (RPV) using an infrared or electro-optical link. Beyond line of sight acquisitions also require real time command and control to hand off targets to the gun or missile that will take them under fire. It is important to note the difference in day and night acquisitions as well as between fair and inclement weather situations.

Platform: The platform is important with respect to survivability, mobility, and agility. Mobility is considered the capability to bring cross hairs to the critical point, whereas agility is the ability to move quickly from point to point in order to avoid enemy fire.

Guidance: Guided anti-armor systems can usually be discussed under two broad concepts; command-to-line-of-sight and terminal homing. Command-to-line-of-sight systems are generally subdivided into tracked beacon and beamrider. In tracked beacon guidance, a tracking device located near the launch point is pointed at the target by the gunner. An infrared (IR) tracker then sees a beacon on the rear of the missile and measures the angular displacement of the missile from the line-of-sight (LOS). If the missile is not on the LOS, an error signal is generated and transmitted to the missile to correct its trajectory. The link between ground and missile may be wire or infrared (IR). For the beam rider guidance, a transmitter which projects a coded beam into space is pointed at the target. If the missile flies out of the beam center, a receiver located at the rear of the missile determines the error and provides a new guidance command to the missile. The trajectory is similar to that for the tracked beacon. Beam rider is conceptually simpler. The need for the command link is eliminated. However, more beam rider functions are performed on board the missile, thus adding to missile complexity, reliability, and cost. The beam rider receiver looks back at the launch point, affording greater protection from external interference. However, the existence of the beam provides a warning which could be a cause for counterfire.

Terminal homing systems potentially offer increased capabilities over current systems, to include: higher first round hit and kill probability, longer standoffs, fire and forget, and simultaneous engagements. Launching requirements in terms of target recognition or identification must be considered to distinguish between friendly and enemy weapons.

The laser semi-active guidance concept involves the use of a narrow beam of pulsed, invisible laser energy to designate a spot on the intended target. Missiles equipped with seekers search for the unique signature of the reflected energy from the designated spot, locks-on, and tracks this spot when it enters their field of view. The laser designator may be man-portable, airborne, or vehicle mounted. The missiles may be fired in the direct or indirect fire mode. A passive homing system, utilizing, for example, an optical contrast seeker or an IR seeker, is a true fire and forget system. However, these systems undoubtedly will have a lower terminal accuracy than a laser semi-active and because of their complexity, will cost much more.

Guidance is the key to systems accuracy (probability of hit). Current guidance systems provide the enemy opportunities for electronic countermeasures, which on today's battlefield assumes more and more importance. Laser systems also will provide the enemy some warning of attack. On the other hand, fire and forget systems could enhance survivability. The guidance system also directly influences propulsion (speed).

Munitions: The bottom line of an anti-armor system is, of course, to kill enemy armored vehicles. Therefore, the lethality of the missile/projectile is vital to overall systems performance since it provides the probability of a kill, given a hit on the target. We had many promising developments in the munitions area.

Thus, in assessing the developmental opportunities for anti-armor systems, we examined line of sight systems in day and night and inclement weather conditions and beyond line of sight systems, paying particular attention to the characteristics of survivability, mobility, maintainability, speed of missile, vulnerability to enemy countermeasures, and probabilities of hit and kill.

Survivability is that which allows combatants to avoid and/or absorb most or all attacks and still be capable of decisively engaging the enemy[4]. The elements of survivability for the military materiel developer are:

> Make it difficult to be detected.
> Make it difficult to be hit when detected.
> Make it difficult to damage when hit.
> Make it easy to repair when damaged.

The XM-1, with its improved armor protection, is a prime example of making a system difficult to damage if hit. Data indicated the XM-1 has a much improved survival capability over the M60A3 from a hit by a SAGGER missile.

The TOW Under Armor (ITV) system was an excellent example of improved survivability. The extended firing system allowed the ITV to be fired from defilade reducing detection and the M113 hull enhanced the TOW crew survivability from the expected heavy enemy preparatory fires. The ITV is an excellent example of improved battlefield mobility. The weapon can be rapidly transported in firing mode from one point to another while still providing the flexibility of dismounting the TOW and firing from the ground if desired. The TOW COBRA and HELLFIRE are also prime examples of increased battlefield mobility.

Again quoting Marshall Grechko in Armed Forces of the Soviet State[3], the Soviet's intend to suppress our anti-armor means to the fullest.

> "For support of an attack, the reliable suppression of the systems of fire of the defense is demanded, especially long range anti-tank means."

With respect to maintainability, a mechanized infantry battalion depended greatly upon the power supply situation for its anti-armor systems and night vision devices. The weakest links in both systems were the batteries. At the time, a European mechanized battalion had over 3,000 batteries, of which 400-plus were rechargeable. By 1985, ten new systems would have entered the inventory, adding over 1,500 batteries, all of which were rechargeable. This would have introduced twelve to fourteen different types of batteries, calling for six to eight different types of chargers, each requiring generators. A review of battery utilization and the equipment authorized to accomplish the mission indicated that we could not get there under current plans. For example, the lack of battery chargers was the main defect in TOW operational readiness of the ARVN in Vietnam in 1974. In late 1977, all concerned (five project managers and four development centers) were hammering out a solution. By 1980, we would hopefully have lithium disposable batteries which would reduce the weight requirements by 50% and increase battery life three times. Nevertheless, the Army would still have many types of batteries. Notwithstanding, night vision devices would still be highly dependent upon the availability of rechargeable Nicad batteries. However, by 1985, it was hoped to have a single standardized disposable lithium battery for use in a mechanized battalion.

The three major anti-tank guided missile systems then in the US Army inventory (Shillelagh, TOW, and DRAGON) bear considerable similarities which impacted on their common susceptibility to countermeasures. All three systems use command to line of sight guidance. We concluded that to optically counter our missile systems the enemy would have to mount a pulsed xenon light to each armored vehicle to be protected, and the xenon light would have to be activated during an attack to provide protection. This did not appear to be feasible.

The current known enemy approach to countering anti-attack systems is through the effective use of smoke and aerosols which obscure the field of view of the missile/tank gunners, or adversely affect the guidance loop between the missile and tracker, thereby forcing the missile to fly an unguided trajectory. It is highly probable, judging from enemy literature and actual maneuver observations that smoke and aerosols will be heavily employed by the enemy in combat operations in an attempt to counter or degrade the effectiveness of optically aimed weaponry.

While there may be some uncertainty concerning the Soviets' use of optical countermeasures there is none concerning his use of smoke and aerosols. Perhaps one of our most important developmental opportunities rested in the development of an effective smoke or aerosol that cannot be penetrated by enemy lasers or passive systems. There is also some indication the enemy anthracene smokes because of their particle size and coloration cannot be penetrated by 10.6 micron FLIR devices. This is an area that required much more knowledge on our part and which is considered vital from offensive and defensive considerations.

We concluded that the next generation missile systems should proliferate guidance systems, provide a faster missile, and have a warhead that will defeat new armor. The laser beam rider appeared to offer the most promising results.

Guided weapons entered combat inventories during World War II and have been used in greater and greater numbers since then. AMSAA conducted a study to obtain a first order estimate of the historical combat effectiveness of guided weapons. Their research indicates the following gross estimates of effectiveness for these weapons with more than 500 combat expenditures.

Table 11
Guided Weapon Combat Effectiveness

TYPE	QUANTITY FIRED	PROB KILL
V-1s ANTWERP	4800+	0.04
V-2s LONDON	1100+	0.45
KAMIKAZE SHIPS	900+	0.05
SA-2 vs US AIRCRAFT	10,000+	0.02
AIM vs SOVIET AIRCRAFT	600+	0.01
ATGM vs TANKS	10,000+	0.01

Source: AMSAA, 1976

To date, the probability of kill in a combat environment has been low for guided weapons. Although we should expect an order of magnitude improvement in effectiveness for new systems, there can be no doubt that our guided weapons will be substantially degraded in effectiveness in combat from the results obtained in a proving ground environment.

Actual field tests by AMSAA indicated that by putting "man in the loop" you get appreciable reductions in the probability of kill. Then when you introduce maneuvering enemy vehicles which present variable sized jinking targets, you get further degradation. Lastly, there are severe problems with intervisibility, the ability of a missile to keep enemy armor in view. BSI and MITRE conducted research into the intervisibility problem and unearthed several fundamental factors which required consideration.

Intervisibility can be defined in space as the existence of any line of sight between a stationary firing position and a moving target; or in time as the interval of time from exposure of a target to a defending gunner until the target again disappears from view. Thus, we have intervisibility distances and intervisibility times. There have been many terrain studies to determine intervisibility. It is interesting to note that when these studies are compared with the same ground resolution between data points, i.e., a reading every twenty-five yards, that there is not that much difference between data taken in the North German Plain, the Fulda Gap, Fort Knox, or in the deserts at Fort Bliss or Fort Irwin. Approximately 50% of the time the visible path length for an armored vehicle is on the order of 150 meters. If we consider that a gunner sees a target the instant it is exposed, intervisibility times can be considered as the sum of the time to fire plus the flight time of a missile. AMSAA field data indicated that the times to fire of all ATGM systems at distances of 3 km. and less is rarely under ten seconds, although it varies somewhat from system to system. If the target disappears before the gunner pulls the trigger you have a missed opportunity to fire and there is no projectile loss. However, if the target disappears from view after firing then you have an abort situation.

Intervisibility is important, then, since it creates missed opportunities to fire, aborted missiles, and with the laser semi-active systems coming on line, it will create problems in laser designation. The bottom line is that an enemy who chooses his terrain carefully will be able to close on our defensive positions, perhaps often within his main gun killing range. The Soviets are extremely conscious concerning the use of terrain and in the use of smoke to assist their forward movement by creating artificial obscurations to visibility.

There are four major factors influencing intervisibility: the time to acquire and fire; the time of flight of the missile; the target speed; and the visible path length (VPL) of the attacker, which depends in some measure on the height of the observer. Each of these factors influences the abort probability, i.e., the probability that once the trigger is pulled, the target will not be there when the missile arrives. For a target averaging 4.5 m/sec at a range of 3.0 km and considering terrain data, a VPL of 150 meters indicates the abort probability for the TOW is about 50% whereas for the supersonic laser beam rider (LBR) it is only half of that. Thus the faster the missile, the less the abort probability. The DRAGON is much less effective at the closer ranges because of its slow velocity. There is also a definite increase in abort probabilities for a faster moving target. In this respect, the XM-1 with its greater agility will have a higher degree of survivability than the M60 or the T-72.

The visible path length is very important. The longer the path, the less the probability of an abort. It is vital for Blue tanks to choose short visible paths as they bound forward. Finally then, is the influence of the time to fire. Although it pays to train gunners to be more effective in acquiring and bringing fires on targets, the payoff is not nearly as great as it is for improved missile velocity. As stated, the laser beam rider will have one-half the abort probability of the TOW.

Laser semi-active weapons used in the line-of-sight battle are currently not very effective. Yet, the Army persisted in ascribing unrealistically high Pks to the Copperhead that were skewing combat effectiveness models, ammo buys, and force structure[5]. The Legal Mix V Study, for example, indicated a Pk of 0.63 and did not consider reduced environmental conditions. It was well past time to strike a note of realism.

Copperhead with a RPV or with other seekers could be combat effective. BSI recommended that development concentrate on the beyond line-of-sight battle and fire and forget seekers in order to insure cost effectiveness of the system. Without a more realistic assessment of the influence of terrain and enemy tactics on target presentation, one could design weapons which considered in isolation show great performance but which would be only of limited value on the battlefield.

You have seen in the 1977 COMCAP war game that Red ATGMs contributed 8% to their total force strength, whereas the Blue ATGMs contributed 20% to the total Blue force strength. Linkage diagrams indicated that the Blue ATGM firepower was directed at the high value Red armored systems. On the other hand, almost all the Red systems attrited the Blue ATGMs (many on one) indicating that it was important to improve Blue ATGM survivability, particularly against Red artillery suppression. The Improved TOW Vehicle would do much to redress that situation.

The Soviets, in analyzing the importance of ATGMs, generally agreed that their ground force component most threatened was the motorized infantry. They were concerned that Blue's use of ATGMs against the BMP would slow the tempo of operations since if the Soviet infantry had to dismount, the tanks would either venture forward without infantry protection or they would have to reduce the speed of attack. Colonel Shapololov, writing in the Military Herald No. 6 in 1975 said[6],

> "Over half of the fifty articles covering the current anti-tank debate have focused on the BMP vulnerability exclusively."

COMCAP 85 bears out their concern because 40% of Blue Values in the war game came from killing the BMP, the same as for killing the M-80. Since war gaming had indicated the importance of the ATGMs versus the highly mechanized Red force it was important to upgrade the ATGM whenever possible. Obviously, the velocity of the DRAGON had to be improved. It was important to provide greater mobility to the ATGM and the Improved Tow Vehicle or similar platforms and the helicopter born HELLFIRE missile which was in development would accomplish that. Of course, the lethality of warheads was very important. The development of a laser beam rider would proliferate the type of guidance making Red electronic countermeasure more difficult. With respect to target acquisition it was important to speed up the development of FLIR devices to provide all-around acquisition capabilities in smoke and at night and in inclement weather.

Because ATGMs have HEAT warheads, are relatively slow, and can currently be encountered by smoke, we have seen the advent of new armor, enhanced agility, and the provision for tank smoke generating devices. Although the Soviets have often indicated they intend to use the cover of smoke and limited visibility conditions to close with our forces, we had not yet developed a land navigation system so essential to maneuver under these circumstances. The Soviets have had such systems on their tanks since 1955. We also knew that laser semi-active systems were now entering both the US and Soviet inventories...yet we had no laser warning systems. ATGMs have influenced new tank designs. That in itself is a major break from the tank-to-tank design tradition of the past thirty years. Later data from the Yom Kippur War has shown that from 7 to 15% of the Arab tank kills were by ATGMs (much less than initially thought), generally in the early part of the war before the Israeli's evolved adequate armor defensive tactics[1].

ATGMs have not sounded the death knell to Armor! In an all-out war this is still the "Age of Armor." The tank is still the dominant battlefield system. However, ATGMs cannot be dismissed lightly. They are accurate, lethal weapons that can be easily transported and proliferated and their life-cycle costs are relatively small. Their presence on the battlefield is important. In fact Soviet Lt Gen. Koritchuck states categorically "The anti-tank guided missile projectile (ATGM) is the basic anti-tank means in contemporary battle."[7]

In all our analyses of the close combat mission area it was always the tank, the infantry fighting vehicle (Bradley), and ATGMs that greatly influenced the outcome of battle, **not the helicopter.**

Any "transformational" efforts to downsize the tank and the IFV to make them lighter and more mobile and transportable must focus upon maintaining their current firepower and survivability capabilities. It would be a tragic error in the design of Future Combat Systems to primarily focus upon counter-insurgency types of conflicts. If that occurs then ATGMs may gain ascendency over armor.

INTELLIGENCE, SURVEILLANCE, AND TARGET ACQUISITION (ISTA)

The ISTA mission area included five functional groups of systems: reconnaissance, surveillance and target acquisition (RSTA), signal intelligence (SIGINT), electronic warfare (EW), strategic intelligence, and intelligence support. ISTA is more easily viewed as a combination of functions which support a variety of missions rather than as a prime mission itself. It is closely related to the overall command and control structure for its organizational aspects and to weapons/sensor capabilities for time and accuracy trade-offs.

Considering the potential Soviet threat in 1975:

- combat would be faster paced, more mobile, and more violent.
- there would be a need to strike targets more selectively and at greater ranges.
- there was a greater variety and sophistication of sensors and weapons.
- there would be a greater prevalence of electronic warfare.
- and there was a requirement for close coordination of ground and air combat.

Our analyses indicated conclusively that the most important function in obtaining an adequate force multiplier against the superior numbered Soviet force in the European environment was the development of a greatly improved ISTA mission area. This was true then and is true today in 2017.

ISTA is a fundamental mission in all degrees of conflict. In the insurgency in Vietnam, US forces had several excellent sensory systems gathering information, but the sensors could not provide the data to the ground forces in time for exploitation because combat units had no downlink receiving capabilities. This lack of time lines was also a major problem limiting war fighting capabilities in both the recent conflicts in Iraq.

The development of an ISTA system includes not only the collection of significant time sensitive combat information and intelligence about an enemy, but also its dissemination from the collection point to the actual users. The collection and dissemination of ISTA data must be related to the effective conduct of tactical operations against the enemy. The importance of combat information is related to the degree to which it affects the three categories of military actions: planning, battle management, and target development.

Planning utilizes intelligence from all sources, tactical and strategic, and considers the battlefield situation in the broadest of terms. Its time line can be from hours to weeks. The data collected is assimilated through a process of complex inferences to estimate probable enemy intentions and to develop plans conditioned upon potential enemy courses of action. Tactical planning is conducted primarily at corps and higher echelons.

Battle management is influenced by the overall planning and must be responsive to the evolving combat situation. It includes such actions as the movement of maneuver elements and the establishment of fire support priorities which utilize both intelligence and combat information. It requires the rapid interpretation of combat information and its time line is generally from minutes to a few hours. Battle management is conducted primarily at division and lower elements.

Target development processes combat information from multiple sources that require immediate responses in order to bring fire, air strikes, and jamming actions upon an engaged enemy. The combat information to be effective must be timely, provide accurate locations, reasonable target identification, and be exploitable by available weapons systems. This response function is almost entirely conducted at brigade and lower echelons and the time line is measured in minutes.

Traditionally, intelligence analysis and the use of reconnaissance and surveillance assets has been guided by the need of intelligence staffs to furnish "intelligence products" in twenty-four hour cycles as input to operational planning rather than by the need to support tactical operations in near-real time. This approach, which is essentially intelligence planning-oriented, and accords with the previous operational doctrine, is best suited to situations in which friendly forces hold the initiative and are, therefore, free to plan the next attack. Target acquisition, under the traditional approach, is primarily left to lower echelon combat forces using information sources and systems which are primarily ground-based and deployed close to the front line and which report directly to them.

Considering probable scenarios in NATO Europe, and taking into account the greatly enhanced capabilities of modern detection and collection systems, there was a clear need to update ISTA employment concepts. War in Europe would probably be initiated by a surprise attack, compelling friendly forces, at least initially, to engage in defensive operations against numerically superior enemy forces. Not only will the enemy have a major numerical advantage, but the Soviet forces had systems of greatly increasing sophistication, particularly in the level of deployed sensor/weapons technology. The entire electronic aspect of warfare had vastly increased. This, coupled with the potential for frequent adverse weather and visibility, further complicates the accomplishment of friendly ISTA missions and attenuated the effectiveness of friendly air and artillery.

The characteristics of the current ISTA systems in 1976 can be succinctly summarized as follows:

- The preponderance of assets were at division level and below
- Reliance was on HUMINT, visual observation, and information generated by lower-level tactical units
- We had non-automated, ground based, line-of-sight limited systems
- The preponderance of data flowed up with varying amounts of filtering
- Systems were structured to support periodic planning
- The output of planning and battle management flowed downward
- The ISTA systems were not organized/equipped to handle the much larger volumes of information to be found in a European environment
- Special Intelligence remained compartmented, preventing the exploitation of its full potential
- Army/Air Force interfaces existed at various levels only for tactical air support and air defense

The question was, how then can the current ISTA System be improved to meet future requirements, particularly the current threat in Europe? A successful defense will depend heavily on the effective use of electronic warfare and on medium and long range electronic surveillance systems to interfere with enemy command, control and communications and to detect enemy vulnerabilities for local exploitation. Given these broad critical objectives, ISTA operations should be directly related to:

- Identifying enemy axes of advance and enemy intentions and capabilities with sufficient detail to allow effective deployment of friendly forces.
- Locating enemy reserve echelons in order to disrupt/destroy and slow speed of advance.
- Determining enemy vulnerabilities to allow seizure of initiatives.

- Supporting near-real time targeting from the FEBA to approximately 30 kms forward of the FEBA.
- Providing commanders with an operations analysis capability which would exploit collected information about the enemy, particularly with respect to enemy vulnerabilities.

The big question was how much information was required about the enemy and then how to react to the information once obtained through ISTA operations. That boiled down to what assets were needed to do the job, determining sensor capabilities and limitations, and obtaining the best balance of systems within the Army and between the Air Force and National systems. Having accomplished that we must determine how to tie them together for operations. In the past, a sensory system was normally developed to fulfill only its particularly designed objective and each was treated as if it were a stand-alone system.

BSI, utilizing the expert assistance of MITRE, analyzed the extremely complex ISTA mission area[8]. In 1976 it consisted of an amalgamation of varying concepts which were generated from studies which were based upon differing premises. Exciting potentials for the application of new technologies existed. To take advantage of new technologies in order to maximize effectiveness, ISTA requirements had to be specified.

The rapid tempo of modern war and the expectation that our forces in Europe would be heavily outnumbered made it important that we should have a continuous picture of enemy activities on the battlefield to provide the capability to maneuver forces and to acquire targets. To meet these requirements many different sensors were currently being developed and were being field tested or operationally deployed. We carefully reviewed all systems in the stages of research, development and procurement. There were nineteen different systems, most of which would not be deployed until the 1980s. These systems included an airborne standoff emitter location system, helicopter-borne surveillance and target acquisition radars, ground based radars for detecting mortar and artillery shells in flight as well as moving personnel and vehicles, unattended ground emplaced sensors for locating enemy artillery.

To sort out the effectiveness of these current and planned systems, it was essential to develop a methodology and employ it to evaluate the relative worth of target acquisition and intelligence systems. We were concerned then with measuring sensory effectiveness in terms of the number of targets that could be detected, classified, identified, and located. We evaluated the

117

sensors in three broad areas: by functional use (target acquisition, cuing, intelligence); by area coverage (Zone 1, Zone 2 A, Zone 2 B); and by target types (movers, shooters, emitters, clusters).

Eight of the nineteen sensors targeted the enemy movers, eight targeted enemy shooters, eleven targeted emitters, and eleven were useful in developing cluster targets. Obviously, several sensors were effective in targeting more than one category of enemy. There were sufficient sensors fielded and in development to have five different suites of sensors covering the four target categories. Which were the most effective? Which, if any, could be eliminated? Which were the most cost effective? To answer those questions we developed a Sensor Effectiveness Index and utilized data inputs from the SCORES war game and existing, planned, or hypothetical sensory parameters targeted against an array of different enemy equipment under varying conditions of terrain, enemy fire suppression, and climate. The results enabled us to take an initial cut at answering the foregoing questions.

Consider that the Soviets had a definitive force ratio advantage and their doctrine called for major artillery suppression fires and armored penetration operating continuously in reduced visibility both at night and in inclement weather with a proliferation of electronic emitters many of which provide an excellent air defense capability. Consequently, with respect to information collection, there will be an order of magnitude increase in the numbers of targets, collection will be at greater ranges, the data will be more comprehensive, and the lower level inputs will no longer of themselves be sufficient. To counter these trends of the mechanization of force, the increased electronic aspect of warfare, the improved level of deployed sensors and weapons technology, and the vastly increased tempo of battle compared to past conflicts, ISTA analysis will have to be rapid, flexible, and timely. That requires that sensor connected, event oriented, closed loop methods of operations be defined for critical tactical actions at each echelon. Therefore, BSI's emphasis focused on relating ISTA data to tactical actions.

One of the inputs to the sensor effectiveness model we developed was the relative value of enemy intelligence targets of various types[9]. For our calculations we chose a Red Army composed of four tank divisions and one motorized rifle division. Data was based upon a SCORES Europe II scenario covering one day of combat. This scenario provided a large number of mobile targets of varied types (tanks, artillery, air defense, etc.) operating in difficult environments (weather, terrain, foliage, etc) utilizing probable enemy countermeasures (jamming, air defense, tactical aircraft).

Blue sensors were required to detect, locate or classify targets within line-of-sight (0 to 5 kms.) and beyond line-of-sight (5 to 50 kms.) in support of planning, ground force maneuver, and target strikes. Our enemy target array included 39 different target types.

The first step was to develop an enemy target list. There were 20 individual targets such as tanks, mortars, trucks, artillery, AA guns, VHF emitters, and acquisition/tracking radars. In the five division enemy force there were 60 motorized rifle companies and 160 tank companies. Consequently we considered ten group targets including armored, missile, mortar and artillery units. We also took into consideration nine different cluster targets such as bivouac areas, command posts, supply points and repair facilities. Cluster targets are generally obtained through inference, correlation and analysis in a fusion process at higher headquarters. All 39 targets were arrayed in accordance with their normal deployment.

Target distribution was a very important element in our model. Each enemy target was located by zone. Zone 1 being 0 to 5 kms. from the FEBA, Zone 2A from 5 to 30 kms., and Zone 2 B from 30 to 50 kms.

The next step was to design a value system in order to determine the relative worth of sensors in acquiring enemy targets[10]. One method was to make these values dependent upon the potential threat that the enemy target might pose. In the COMCAP studies previously discussed the value of an attrition producing weapon in the central duel was proportionate to the value of the targets killed by that weapon in a given time, i.e., the weapons effectiveness value (WEV). Recall that the WEVs were obtained by a normalizing process which in COMCAP 77, for example, related all weapons value to the US M60A-3 tank which had a value of 1.0.

We chose ten enemy weapons systems involved in the central duel (T-62 tank, BMG, SSM, SAM, mortar, artillery, multiple rocket launcher, anti-tank gun, anti-tank missile, AA gun). When the total number of these Red weapons involved in the central duel were multiplied by their respective WEVs obtained in the COMCAP studies we arrived at the total Red force effectiveness in the central duel, which was 2040.

Values of the other ten individual weapons such as the Red acquisition/tracking radars were obtained in relation to their support of the central duel. For example, it was considered that the 349 acquisition/tracking radars were worth about 75% of the value of the weapons they supported. The 245 SAMs (WEV = 1.15) had a total value of 340 and the 80 AA guns (WEV = 0.16) had a total value of 13. Thus:

$$\text{V radar } (349) = .75\ (340 + 13)$$
$$\text{V radar} = .76$$

The ten group targets were computed by adding up the value of the individual targets in the group. A Red Tank Company comprised of ten tanks and one truck had a value as shown:

$$\text{V tank company} = 10\ (.38) + 1\ (.05) = 3.85$$

To determine the value of cluster targets we related them to the total force effectiveness (2040) in the central duel. For example, if 20% of the Red force was estimated to be in 145 different assembly areas in Zone 2A and 2B then:

$$\text{V assembly area x } 145 = 0.20 \text{ x } 2040$$
$$\text{V assembly area} = 2.81$$

To the extent that Red individual weapons were considered to be in group or cluster targets care was taken not to double count. For example, those Red tanks judged to be in a company formation were subtracted from the total number of individual tank targets. Further, if there were three tank companies in an assembly area, then similar reductions in tank company targets as well as in individual tanks had to be accounted for.

To facilitate analysis, all Red equipment was classified as movers, shooters, emitters, and cluster targets. Emitters were further broken down into two categories: communications equipment, such as a HF radio and VHF single channel radio; and non-communications equipment, such as ground support radars, jammers, and acquisition/tracking radars.

Examples of the distribution of the 39 different Red targets in the three zones being considered and their relative values are given in Table 12.

Table 12
Examples of Red Target List

	Type	Number by Zone 1 / 2A / 2B	Relative Value
MOVERS	Tank	328/645/688	.38
	Command Vehicle	26/44/32	.55
SHOOTERS	Artillery	0/421/0	.18
	AA Gun	24/24/32	.16
	Tank	328/0/0	.38
EMITTERS	HF Radio	1139/476/85	.05
	VHF Multi-channel	0/20/83	.50
	Acq/Tracking Radar	24/132/193	.76
	Communication Jammer	10/10/4	2.80
CLUSTERS	Unit CP	18/81/64	2.98
	Assembly areas	0/81/64	2.81
	Repair Facilities	0/15/22	0.75

Unquestionably, there are many possible methods of determining relative target values and this method was just one of them.

There are many factors affecting the performance of a sensor system, such as sensor activity, target activity, timeliness, accuracy, periodicity, area covered, survivability, jamming, weather, darkness, terrain, completeness, and geographic overlap. All of which were inputs to our sensor effectiveness methodology. We applied our methodology in one target type, a group of target types, and all target types, depending upon the end use of the data. MITRE developed a Sensor Effectiveness Index (SEI) to evaluate the performance of various sensors utilizing the developed Red target values.

SEI = Sum of all target types times the fraction of targets reported in a given interval times the target value times the information use factor.

Where: The fraction of targets reported in a time interval was equal to the number of targets available to the sensor times the fraction detected and reported in the required interval under ideal conditions times the environmental reduction due to jamming, darkness or weather observation.

The number of targets available to the sensor was the number of active targets times the fraction of time the sensor was active (periodicity), which depended upon the operational limitations of the sensor system.

The target values were as previously discussed.

The information use factor (the value of information) depended upon whether the acquired enemy target location was good enough for targeting (shooting) 50m, cuing 500 m, or intelligence 5000m. The time line threshold was 30 seconds for targeting, two minutes for cuing , and 60 minutes for intelligence.

The information use factor is a function of the utilization of target information and is strictly a subjective input. We used several different alternatives. One was to assign quality values based upon the utilization of information independent of the zone where the target was identified, that is:

Targeting	.67
Cuing	.27
Intelligence	.06

Another was to apply a different information use factor for each zone, for example:

	Targeting	Cuing	Intelligence
Zone 1	10	5	1
Zone 2A	10	7	2
Zone 2B	6	5	3

To measure the effectiveness of sensors in battle it was necessary to make value judgements in the scenario including Red capabilities, Red target values, and the utilization of the target information. Our system allowed us to vary the inputs and to calculate the relative worth of the 19 sensors under many different situations for their ability to generate targets. We considered three phases of combat: a meeting engagement, a major enemy offensive, and an enemy penetration. Interestingly, even though we varied target values, the information use factor, and combat conditions, the rank ordering of our sensors did not vary significantly. Again, a word of caution concerning the use of numbers in systems analysis is necessary. Numbers are generally never hard and often can be misleading. It is the trends and relative values that count.

In summary, target generation was a function of:
- Number of targets
- Number of active enemy targets
- Fraction of targets in view
- Fraction of time sensor was active
- Reductions for environmental factors and jamming
- Number reported in the required time

Sensor systems were most effective when they:
- Detected a large number of targets
- Had a high look rate
- Discriminated adequately
- Reported in a timely fashion
- Avoided jamming, and
- Survived

Consider as an example the basic sensor profile for the PPS-5 ground support radar (GSR):
- 22 deployed per Division
- Covers Zone 1 completely
- Each radar on 90% of the time
- Enemy action reduces effectiveness to 70%
- Weather reduces effectiveness to 90%
- Smoke and darkness do not affect system
- Enemy jamming reduces effectiveness to 80%
- Irregularities in terrain obscure 50% of Zone 1

The target-sensor relationship between a Red tank and a PPS-5 is as follows:
- 99 single look probability of seeing tank in Zone 1
- Sensor scans each .035 minute
- Targets active 50% of time

- Sensor classifies target as tracked vehicle
- Target location error is +/- 50 m in Zone 1
- Target reported to user 5 minute after detection

In gross terms, the combined results of all nineteen sensors for one set of conditions indicated that the average distribution of enemy target values were as follows[11]:

Table 13
Average Distribution of Target Values

Target Categories		Sensor Information		Distribution	
Movers	6%	Shootable	17%	Zone 1	24%
Shooters	24%	Cuing	31%	Zone 2a	49%
Emitters	40%	Intelligence	52%	Zone 2b	26%
Cluster	30%				

As discussed previously, the enemy massed his forces at the FEBA where the central duel was fought. It was there that we had to kill the enemy. The sensor array was not finding a great number of targetable (shootable) enemy movers and shooters in Zone 1. There were three major drawbacks; the timing of the receipt of sensor data to the weapons; the reduction of the sensor effectiveness due to enemy fire suppression and inclement weather; and inherent inaccuracies in the sensor information.

Half of the sensors delivered information in sufficient time for targeting less than 10% of the time. One-third of the sensors had the mean value of detecting one target less than 50% of the time. As a result for targeting, only seven sensors had the probability of detecting a target and delivering information to the action source 50% of the time. Obviously, large improvements were required!

With respect to timeliness, the key missing elements were procedures and communications. Currently emphasis was on hardware. There was a lack of concepts and as a result requirements were murky. Technological hardware breakthroughs were enabling sensors to improve target location errors, and sensors were identifying and classifying enemy targets deep into Zone 2. It was the software that was lacking. Application functions for target data routing had to be specified along with the functions of formatting, translation, and inferences. Only then could the basic concept of utilizing combat information for effecting the real time execution of target data routing and the maneuver of forces.

A summary of the factors degrading the performance of the nineteen sensors 20% or more was: [12]

Table 14
Sensor Degradation

Factor	Number of Sensors
Survivability	15
Timeliness	14
Sensor Activity	9
Terrain	9
Accuracy (< 150m)	9
Weather	5
Light Conditions	1

Major increases in sensor effectiveness could be obtained by increasing the survivability of sensors from enemy suppressive fire and electronic counter measures (ECM), particularly for the SOTAS and field artillery acoustic locating system (FAALS), both of which were under development. It was doubtful whether the SOTAS, which had a stand-off helicopter platform, could survive in its present configuration in a European conflict. The requirement for a moving target radar was vital and possibly a more serviceable platform (Air Force) could be obtained.

The major limitations of many of the current systems were: the relatively poor location accuracy at long ranges; the long time delays in processing and distributing data to strike systems; the susceptibility of sensors to relatively small jammers; and the limited coverage beyond the FEBA in Zone 2B.

To overcome these limitations there were potential improvements in the next generation of sensor systems (1985) such as:

- Long range radar and emitter location sensors with precision accuracy to detect targets in Zone 2B.
- RPV and drone platforms to penetrate high threat areas while providing long endurance, high altitude, mask free coverage.
- Improved jam resistant data links and improved digital processing to overcome delays.
- Precision common grid to improve location accuracy and facilitate the handing of targets to strike systems.

Yet there will be residual deficiencies in the next generation of sensor systems. Many of the all-weather stand-off systems have a limited classification capability, non-emitting targets standing in foliage will be difficult to detect and platform survivability and sensor exploitability will still be concerns.

To illustrate the results of individual sensors, we chose four sensors that when operated as a suite together would provide excellent effectiveness.

1) A A communications emitter location system concept under development which is accurate, has continuous coverage, low vulnerability, wide area coverage, and a large target population.

2) B A stand-off target acquisition system in development utilizing a moving target radar (MTR) to find movers which is accurate, has continuous coverage, is vulnerable and has wide area coverage.

3) C A radar system that can locate shooters which is accurate, has continuous coverage, and is vulnerable.

4) D A fielded system that locates non-communication emitters which is accurate, has continuous coverage, medium vulnerability, and limited area coverage.

The subsequent data is for one scenario:

Table 15
Sensor Values for Targeting Purposes

Sensor	No. of Target Types	Probability of Detecting One Target (Mean Value)	Percent Delivered in time (Mean Value)	Effect of Enemy Action Percent
A	35	.67	.80	.85
B	22	.77	.60	.37
C	8	.70	.50	.56
D	5	.90	.76	.66

Table 16
Sensor Worth By Target Type

Sensor	Mover	Shooter	Commun-icator	Non-Comm.	Cluster	Total
A	-	-	504	-	1287	1791
B	291	-	-	-	806	1097
C	-	270	-	-	-	270
D	-	-	-	171	-	171
TOTAL	291	270	504	171	2093	3329

Ten of the nineteen sensors had a worth value less than 130.

Table 17
Sensor Worth By Zone

Sensor	I	IIa	IIb	Total
A	138	565	1088	1791
B	91	501	505	1097
C	1	269	-	270
D	62	24	85	171
TOTAL	292	1359	1678	3329

Table 18
Sensor Worth By Information Use

SENSOR	Targeting 50m	Cuing 500m	Intelligence 5000m	Total
A	392	681	718	1791
B	318	380	399	1097
C	60	97	113	270
D	24	39	108	171
TOTAL	794	1197	1338	3329

Notice for this suite of sensors they still were not particularly effective in targeting enemy movers and shooters in the very important Zone 1 where close combat takes place.

Although sensor effectiveness is of paramount importance in procuring ISTA systems, costs also must be considered. Since several of the intelligence gathering systems were operated at corps level we determined the procurement costs per corps of the systems we analyzed. We then divided the total cost per system by the computed worth of enemy targets identified in order to obtain the cost per unit value.

Table 19
Sensory Cost per Unit Value

SYSTEM	COST/UNIT VALUE (K)
A	69
B	40
C	127
D	143

It was interesting to note that the FAALS (26), RPV Flir (33) and PPS-5 (35) systems had the lowest cost/unit value. The OV-1 (717) and precision locating systems for the suppression of enemy air defense (886) had extremely high costs per unit value. The precision emitter location system under development showed great promise in detecting enemy non-communication emitters and its cost/unit was 107.

The sensors under development and in research showed promise for the future but would not be fielded for several years (the mid 1980's). A comparison of a particularly effective suite of these sensors under development that to the most effective suite of sensors currently in the field or in final development in 1977 indicated that the developmental sensors were generally more effective than the fielded sensors although the overall cost per corps was about double. Obviously, developmental activities for that suite should be continued, although the counter-vulnerability for several systems had to be improved. Sensors targeting shooters still required more attention. It is doubtful that the intelligence gathering capabilities of the OV-1 justifies the expenditures. More thought should be given to the use of RPVs.

As we reviewed the capabilities of sensors I became more and more convinced of the potential effectiveness of RPVs. Of all the sensors reviewed, RPVs had the best chance of survivability on the modern battlefield. They could cover Zone II, classify targets, operate at night, and be developed to destroy targets. I felt that this was a grossly under-funded area of research. In 1977, Dr. Edmund Teller, who was a member of several DOD Advisory Boards, desired to discuss future Army weapons developments. I met with him one-on-one for three hours, fully expecting him to discuss the utilization of his newly developed "clean" nuclear weapon. However, interestingly, the major topic of conversation was the future utilization of RPVs. We both agreed that RPVs had important functions on the battlefield, both for reconnaissance and weapons delivery.

The ISTA systems under development and the improved currently fielded systems were creating a veritable bow wave of target volumes. Target volumes were expected to increase from about 15 targets per minute in 1976 to about 80 targets per minute in 1983 and were expected to increase greatly in the future. Of interest at the time was the fact that 73% of the targets were to be collected by the SIGINT systems of the Army Security Agency. The number of targets collected by the division artillery target acquisition systems improved somewhat and there was projected to be an order of magnitude increase in the collection of targets by division intelligence sources. The dissemination of this increased target volume from sensors to using units was a potential problem of the greatest importance. The paths which information must take from the collection point to the users of information had to be determined and the means developed to insure timely dissemination. We believed that a limited number of basic time-sensitive tactical actions represented the major requirement for effective sensor data dissemination[13]. We identified eight tactical action threads which fit the criteria of encompassing a major portion of the ISTA information requirements, functions and interrelationships from sensors to weapons systems. They were:

-       Control of maneuver elements in battle.
-       Suppression of enemy artillery.
-       Suppression of enemy air defenses.
-       Interdiction of enemy formations in Zones 2 and 3.
-       Destruction/suppression of moving targets in Zones 1 and 2.
-       Degradation of enemy C^3.
-       Determination of enemy main threats and plans of attack.
-       Defense against air penetration.

Each tactical action thread analysis would consider the critical vulnerabilities or targets in the enemy forces addressed by the action and would determine the critical information needs and key decision nodes for executing the action as a basis for establishing systems parameters. Systems parameters would be described in terms of the number of users and their functions, required interfaces between users, and such factors as data volumes and rates, the processing required, and presentation requirements. Alternative configurations to process and distribute this information in support of the individual tactical action should also be considered. Important considerations in developing a system are: current and programmed sensors system capabilities; communications implementation; automated processing support; cost aspects; and survivability and operational performance. The aggregate information needs and systems parameters to support a set of tactical actions would become the design requirements.

Tactical action threads[14] which considered the criticality of enemy targets to be attacked, the time from detection to strike, and the relationship between detection accuracy and weapons capability could be oriented toward finding those detect-strike configurations which required minimal development time, effort and costs. In particular there was an urgent requirement to field effective means to destroy or degrade enemy forward air defense units, jammers, and critical command and communications links. EW warfare had to be capable of more than just locating and jamming the enemy emitters.

Previous analyses had indicated that the two major vulnerabilities of the Soviets were command and control and the mobility of the second echelon forces. Consider that 50% of the enemy's command posts (CPs) and about 90% of enemy artillery units and jammers could be expected to be near the FEBA within the range of friendly artillery. Current SIGINT systems could detect and locate enemy emitters with target location errors (TLE) of about 400 meters, and the new systems being considered should have TLEs of less than 100 meters. It would be most effective to couple the EW systems with a strike capability. Effective strike mechanisms could be terminal homing weapon such ARMs which could home in on enemy emitters and RPVs with homing devices.

The tactical action thread for the degradation of enemy C^3 determined the critical vulnerabilities of Soviet command and control, artillery, air defense, and EW systems, that is, those nodes which when destroyed would create a significant degradation of the enemy combat effectiveness. For example, the command and control of a Soviet air defense Battalion has 37 nodes of which only 6 are critical. By selective targeting, the reduction of enemy effectiveness could be catastrophic, whereas the random destruction of enemy equipment would be graceful. Not only is selective targeting highly effective but it is much more efficient in that it greatly degrades enemy combat power with the least expenditure of munitions. In the SCORES scenario, 80% of the acquired enemy air defense systems, each of which has radar as an integral part of the system, were located within 12 to 16 kilometers of the FEBA, well within friendly artillery range. An anti-radiation artillery projectile that can guide to the source of radar energy represents a potential fire and forget system that would be a significant improvement in air defense suppression capabilities.

The main closed loops tactical action threads where an action cycle can operate in accordance with a commander's policies without involving the TOC in specific decisions are air defense, fire support and EW jamming. "Closed loop" means the existence of an information collection-decision-action chain for the accomplishment of a single battlefield task.

Currently in the absence of standard communication links and data formats the users have to provide dedicated facilities and special operating procedures to handle the outputs of each individual system. Obviously an integrated system to provide a composite target picture of enemy ground movement in real time was required. The netting of radars was possible because of advances in sensor signal processing. MITRE prepared a study to implement the netting concept utilizing new communications technology...the Joint Tactical Information Distribution System (JTIDS). The sensor weapons time lines were definitely a function of communications and procedures and particularly of an information distribution system[15].

Major considerations resulting from our ISTA sensory system analysis were:

- Push the development of emitter locating systems
- Increase the priority of FAALS.
- Systems that detect enemy movers and shooters required more attention.
- It is questionable whether the intelligence use justified the OV-1 systems.
- The survivability of sensor systems must be improved.
- Give more thought to the utilization of RPVs.
- Available technology offered significant future potentials.
- Technology applications must be tied to operational capabilities, such as anti-radiation projectiles.
- A tactical information distribution system was required.

The ISTA systems coming on line portended great increases in capabilities. Take for example the critical function of target acquisition. The following table indicates major improvements in both the ability to acquire targets and the target location error[16].

Table 20
Target Acquisition Performance Comparison

PARAMETERS	1976	1980s	IMPROVEMENT FACTOR
TLE (Target Location Error)	400 Meters	100 Meters	4.0
ACQUISITION PERCENT:			
TRACKED VEHICLES	6 Percent	95 Percent	15.8
ARTILLERY	21 Percent	88 Percent	4.2
WHEELED VEHICLES	4 Percent	36 Percent	9.0

The determination of an effective sensor mix depends upon the: types of enemy targets; distribution and value of targets; sensory capabilities; mission profiles; degradation of sensors; and information use factors.

The aforementioned factors will vary with the type of warfare. In attempting to determine the optimum sensor mix for target acquisition in Central Europe against Warsaw Pact forces you could say:

- There is an enhanced capability to depict the enemy.
- There will be a large increase in combat information.
- We will need redundant sensors.
- Sensor survivability is a problem.
- Time lines must be improved (closed loops), and
- Interservice cooperation is essential.

In summary, technology is providing improved sensors, high speed processing, and distributed communications while offering real time target acquisition and command and control which requires enhanced battlefield systems management.

Unquestionably, in the future, success of battle will greatly depend upon superior information flow. ISTA is closely related to the overall command and control structure for its organizational aspects and the necessity for improved communications and procedures will be discussed subsequently.

COMMAND AND CONTROL

Technology and rapidly changing requirements have led to a large number of ISTA battlefield systems. These systems have sometimes been fielded without well-defined functional interfaces or an overall concept of their battlefield usefulness. Maximum utilization of these systems can only be obtained if they are operated in an integrated battlefield system where all interfaces are clearly defined. Weapons and sensor systems effectiveness depends upon the development of integrated command and control systems. Dr. Malcolm Currie, in a statement to the 94th Congress, said[17],

> "I believe the development of integrated intelligence and target engagement systems represents the great challenge and opportunity for the next decade for DOD....In this connection improved command and control can be regarded as a powerful 'force level multiplier'."

The command and control mission area includes six functional groups of systems: position location, strategic communications, tactical communications, communication security, automation, and other C3.

What is Command and Control?

JCS Publication 1 states, "The exercise of authority and direction by a properly designated commander over assigned forces in the accomplishment of his mission. Command and control functions are performed through an arrangement of personnel, equipment, communications, facilities, and <u>procedures</u> (emphasis added) which are employed by a commander in planning, directing, coordinating, and controlling forces and operations in the accomplishment of his mission."

Command functions are generally concerned with planning, assessing both friendly and enemy capabilities, allocating resources and committing forces. These functions require the gathering, collating, and processing of a large amount of <u>intelligence</u> information that enables commanders to estimate the situation and to make decisions. Control, on the other hand, involves decision making utilizing more specific real-time combat <u>information</u> in order to direct combat action toward defined objectives. The emphasis between command functions and control functions differs at each level of command. As indicated in Chart 26, the emphasis at brigade and lower levels is almost all on combat information whereas at echelons above corps the emphasis is on intelligence. The crossover occurs between division and corps. With respect to ISTA/command and control issues the

Chart 26

COMMAND AND CONTROL

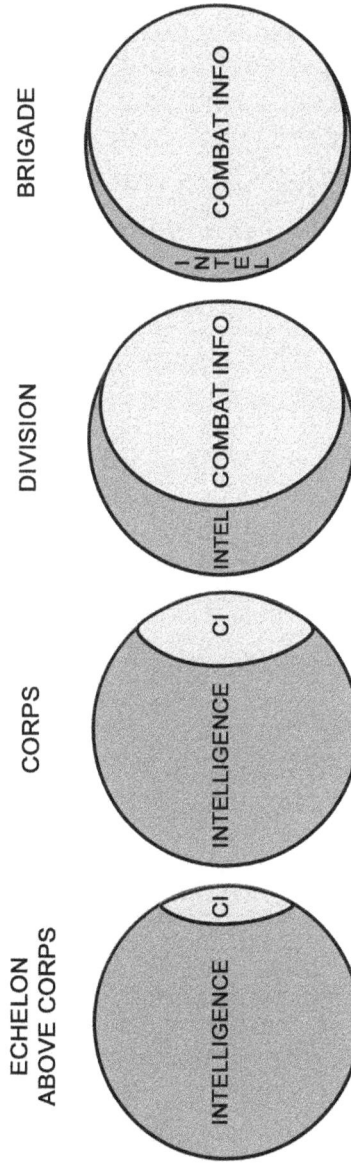

| ECHELON ABOVE CORPS | CORPS | DIVISION | BRIGADE |

- ECHELON ABOVE CORPS: INTELLIGENCE / CI
- CORPS: INTELLIGENCE / CI
- DIVISION: INTEL / COMBAT INFO
- BRIGADE: INTEL / COMBAT INFO

Source: Office of Battlefield Systems Integration/MITRE, 1977

135

organizational line of responsibilities at the time were undergoing major revisions[18].

A single ISTA sensor could support several different applications executed at different echelons so that combat effectiveness depended upon the speed at which information was routed to action centers for decisions and execution. Therefore organizational processing and communications are important, requiring flexibility and rapid data processing.

We recognized that tactical concepts were evolving at a fairly rapid pace and in order to effect a flexible system design we attempted to identify these evolving concepts as they differentiated between corps and division operations[19]. They were as follows:

Table 21
Evolving Concepts[20]

Division	Corps
• Closed Loop	• Intelligence Fusion
• Combat Information	• All Source Information
• Metal on Target	• Plan, Coordinate Fires
• Real Time Graphics	• Future Intent
• Highly Mobile	• Move Infrequently
• Compact ADP	• Suitable Data Bases
• Limited Personnel	• Op and Intel Analysts
• Minimize Interfaces	• Tactical and Strategic Interfaces

All of the ISTA sensors required varying amounts of processing of the raw sensor information into a form useable by tactical data systems. The sensor processing function could be integral to the sensor itself as is the case with the AN/TPQ-37 or a separately identifiable station as is the case with the SOTAS. Processed information from different families of sensors was integrated at various tactical data system (TDS) locations prior to further dissemination. At the time several tactical data systems such as TOS, TACFIRE and CAC had already been fielded but as yet there was no program to address the development of a comprehensive targeting or analysis capability.

A simplified schematic of the then current tactical data systems (TDS) is shown on Chart 27. Note that there are five major data input sources into the division tactical operations center (DTOC). These are:

1) Artillery inputs were provided by TACFIRE, the artillery TDS, which was an integrated system of digital computers, input/output devices and digital storage and retrieval devices. TACFIRE was designed to perform automatic data processing associated with field artillery functions that would improve the effectiveness of artillery fire support.

2) SIGINT inputs were provided by the ASA operated Control and Analysis Center (CAC) which received data for all SIGINT and EW sensor systems. CACs were planned for theater, corps, and division levels. CACs contained computer driven systems designed to provide management and direction to SIGINT/EW systems and to correlate sensor data. The divisional operated sensors at time were Teampack for SIGINT and Trailblazer for COMINT.

3) The Corps TOC received inputs from the air force and theater sensor systems: the air defense command and control system which processed long range radar and aircraft track data and disseminated the data and commands to SAM firing units; and the corps CAC which had sensors for ELINT and COMINT. The division utilized the CTOC and corps assets to perform many of the less time critical functions.

4) The Moving Target Locators were the network sensors comprised of GSRs and REMBASS which provided all weather information on enemy movements beyond the FEBA in a division's area of interest, and SOTAS. SOTAS utilizing a MTI radar was to be employed to detect, locate and track enemy vehicles and personnel. As discussed previously, these moving target locators should be integrated into a separate TDS.

5) Units in contact provided information on both enemy and friendly units and activities.

Chart 27

TACTICAL DATA SYSTEMS

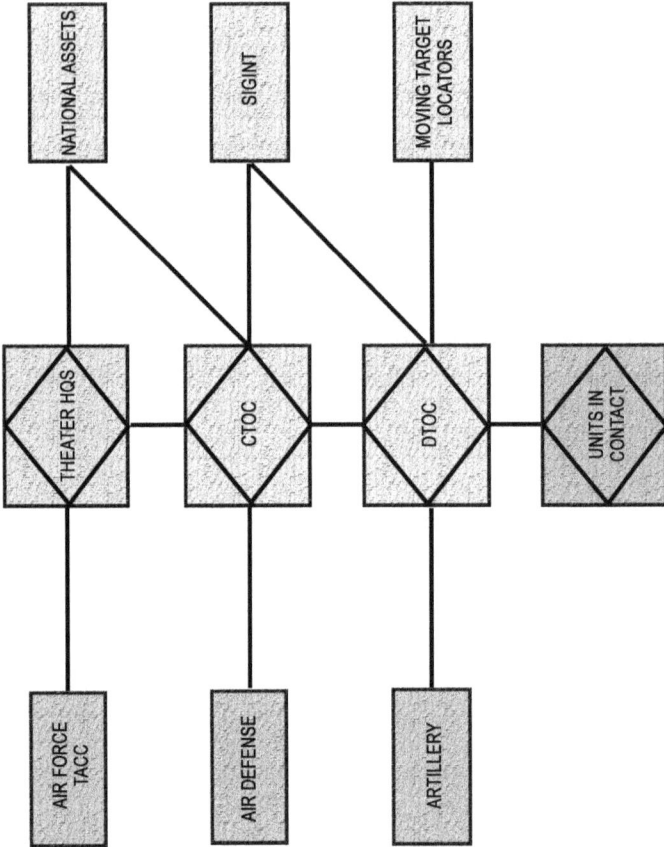

Source: Office of Battlefield Systems Integration/MITRE, 1977

Information from the aforementioned five sources (TACFIRE, CAC, CTOC, moving target sensors and units in contact) was routed to the DTOC where the tactical operations systems (TOS) was located. TOS was a computer oriented command and control system whose objective was to enhance the capability of ground combat commanders to manage the employment of Army combat power. Emphasis has been placed on G-2/G-3 staff functions and software applications of the friendly and enemy situations.

Recognizing that these tactical data systems required a systems concept for the utilization of multi-source intelligence and target acquisition information to provide real-time target engagement and a fusion of this information at the corps and division levels to facilitate timely and accurate maneuver decisions, BSI/MITRE developed a Target and Acquisition Control System (TACS)[21]. TACS encompassed those corps and below tactical data systems and sensors which contributed to intelligence collection and target acquisition, processing of data, fire support, and the control and coordination of combat forces.

TACS was a concept for integrating the flow of information within the corps and the division in accordance with four basic principles:

1.   Timely information was needed by the corps and division commanders and their staffs in order to plan operations, to direct maneuver units, and to put fire power on selected targets, all in accordance with the pace of modern combat.

2.   All information showing the location of current probable enemy activity would be transmitted in near real-time to appropriate users.

3.   Information from all sources would be correlated in near real-time in the corps and division tactical operations center.

4.   In addition to immediate transmission to the TOC, information on selected targets or categories of targets, delivered directly to TACFIRE or other appropriate weapons control systems would make it possible for those targets to be engaged immediately.

The TACS information interfaces were derived from current division and field artillery doctrine and the basic principles stated above. In almost all cases, the interconnecting links were bi-directional and in general, target intelligence information flowed inward and orders/control/directions flowed outward.

To summarize, the TACS concept for an automated coordination system was that all source, real-time, formatted information be sent to dispersed elements by multiple access data exchanges thus reducing vulnerabilities and permitting immediate actions.

To date (1976), the Army's efforts to automate support for command systems functions, the tactical Operations System (TOS), had not been successful. TOS was not designed to satisfy evolving concept requirements and attempts for TOS to meet those requirements would require significant modifications. TOS emphasized intelligence and operational analysis and planning and could not utilize real-time inputs for targeting. It was doubtful to us at the time if the current configuration of TOS would ever be successful in providing the commander with a real-time picture of enemy movement, timely maneuver information or the ability to attrit and delay the enemy by fire. Technology had advanced sufficiently to permit the fielding of a powerful and flexible test bed geared to the evolving tactical concepts and the advent of real-time sensor interfaces. TOS should have been deep-sixed earlier since it had no targeting capabilities.

BSI/MITRE expended great efforts in analyzing the Army's current relatively unresponsive command and control systems.

The basic command and control functions were[22]:
- Dynamic force management (commanding).
- Real-time data handling (targeting).
- Interoperability.
- Security and Survivability.

Dynamic force management is the requirement for flexible, fast, precise information processing. The dominant need appeared to be for information displays and decision making aids for rapid assessments and decisions.

Real-time data handling required sensor source data automation, most likely utilizing thresholding and exception reporting techniques. Communication processing was a key element and new tactical information data systems were required. Sensor processing had to be expedited by using algorithms to extract useful data. Finally, in order to exploit the super abundance of input data coming on line multisource data fusion was essential, particularly at higher echelons. To summarize the requirement for real time data handling, highly perishable data inputs must be received, communicated, processed, and fused in order to exploit targets as well as to permit an accurate and useful reflection of reality for dynamic force management.

The basis of interoperability is the commander's operational concept. From that, information flow requirements could be determined and an interface management plan adopted at corps and above levels. Potential joint and combined applications should be addressed. Interoperability must be considered early in the process to avoid costly retrofits.

Both security and survivability are important in a command and control system. With respect to security, multi-user time shared, remotely accessible inputs lead to over compartmentalization. On the other hand for survivability data fusion and processing requirements lead to over centralization.

The question of operating mode as well as organization must be answered. Do we provide front line units the means to detect, select and shoot targets in real time or do we opt for a more centralized collection system, say at corps, with target hand-offs? In an article prepared in 1976 for the New York Times, General Westmoreland said[23],

> "The increased threat of tactical surprise has generated two chains of logic as how best to meet this threat, one stressing decentralization and the other centralization. These chains of logic are superficially opposed to one another and each has its proponents. Therefore, some disarray in current thinking about the future battlefield has inhibited decisive action to prepare for the future."

Organizational aspects were still undecided which led BSI to the conclusion that a flexible command and control test bed was absolutely essential to determine the most logical solution to the centralization conundrum.

With respect to tactical data systems we found that hardware is not the problem; software is often late, costly, and non-responsive; requirements change; and change must be part of the plan.

Technology was increasing at a rapid rate, so that rather than concentrating on hardware, which many developers were prone to do, stress should be placed on procedures. We found a lack of concepts, mushy requirements, and a general insufficient familiarity with data systems at all levels.

The problem of changes in response to user needs is endemic to command and control. Understandably, user requirements often change due to changes in policy, doctrine and organization. However, the lack of user involvement in critical development phases spawns unrealistic requirements and systems development by technicians leaving no opportunities for design validation. Because doctrinal requirements for command and control were evolving concepts it was absolutely essential that there be continuous user/developer interfaces. Command and control systems are generally difficult to change because of inflexible software, normally poor documentation and the magnitude of maintenance requirements.

The cost drivers for developing tactical data systems have changed dramatically. Whereas hardware used to be the major cost element, costs are now driven strictly by software development. Consequently new techniques and management practices are necessary. Modular design, top down structural programming and continuous visibility are necessary in order to be able to effect inevitable user changes. Tactical systems software development should;

- integrate software first
- improve the visibility of software development process
- solve tough problems early
- develop flexible design
- maintain rigid control of development
- be introduced to the field incrementally.

BSI worked hand in glove with the Commanding General of Fifth Corps in Germany[24] assisting in solving his tactical command and control problems.[25] As we saw it, the major issues were:

- to provide some capability to units in the field in near term
- integrate the sensor information that will be available in the near term
- respond to the evolving tactical concepts for command and control
- to support the tactical commander.

The aforementioned issues could be satisfied by developing a flexible command and control test bed. A flexible test bed would provide an early demonstration of tactical C^3. Sensors could also be integrated to provide commanders with real-time data. The test bed would provide essential continuity between the user and developer thereby allowing the merger of software applications and interfaces with engineering development hardware.

Consequently, BSI contracted with The Federal Systems Division of the International Business Machine Corporation to define an integrated, highly responsive set of real-time command and control applications at the division, the division Real-Time Applications Specifications Program

(DIVRAS)[26]. Efforts by TRADOCs Combined Arms Center and BSI had led to an emerging concept for a division automation center which allowed the DTOC to accommodate organizationally and procedurally the large number of real time information sources coming on line. Two of the basic building blocks for the DIVRAS system were TACS and the concept of closed loop systems previously discussed. The main features of the division automation system are shown in Chart 28. Rather than emphasizing hardware as in the past, the immediate goal of the DIVRAS program was to specify the application functions for the target data routing and a simplified commander display in support of fire and maneuver. DIVRAS emphasized procedures rather than hardware.

The three major areas of investigation were:

1. Information Flow and Interoperability Analysis, to develop a battlefield scenario, analyze information flow, and determine message traffic and content for combat information reaching the DTOC.
2. Target Data Routing Analysis, to develop target data algorithms to support the analysis of fire missions. Procedures were established to translate, infer, filter, correlate, associate, and assign information.
3. Commanders Maneuver Display Analysis, to develop a map background and the symbology requirements for a simplified commander display which would allow the commander to utilize all the available real time data on enemy movers, shooters, and emitter locations.

The DIVRAS automation system considered the five principal sources of combat information flowing into the DTOC which were previously discussed. These included the outputs from 13 ISTA sensor systems. The need for system integration and the determination of information flow requirements and an interface management plan can readily be understood when it is realized that in a single division area there were currently authorized and planned 45 separate sensor tactical data system vans.

The key to the real-time DIVRAS concept was the sensory sources providing data on enemy "Movers, Shooters and Emitters." For targeting applications, target intelligence from mover, shooter, and emitter reports together with photint and fused intelligence from corps was merged automatically at the DTOC and routed to appropriate weapons systems. For maneuver display, the commander was presented a simplified, threat oriented portrayal of the battlefield situation which allowed him to utilize all of the available real-time data. The commander's display presentation

Chart 28

DIVISION AUTOMATION SYSTEM

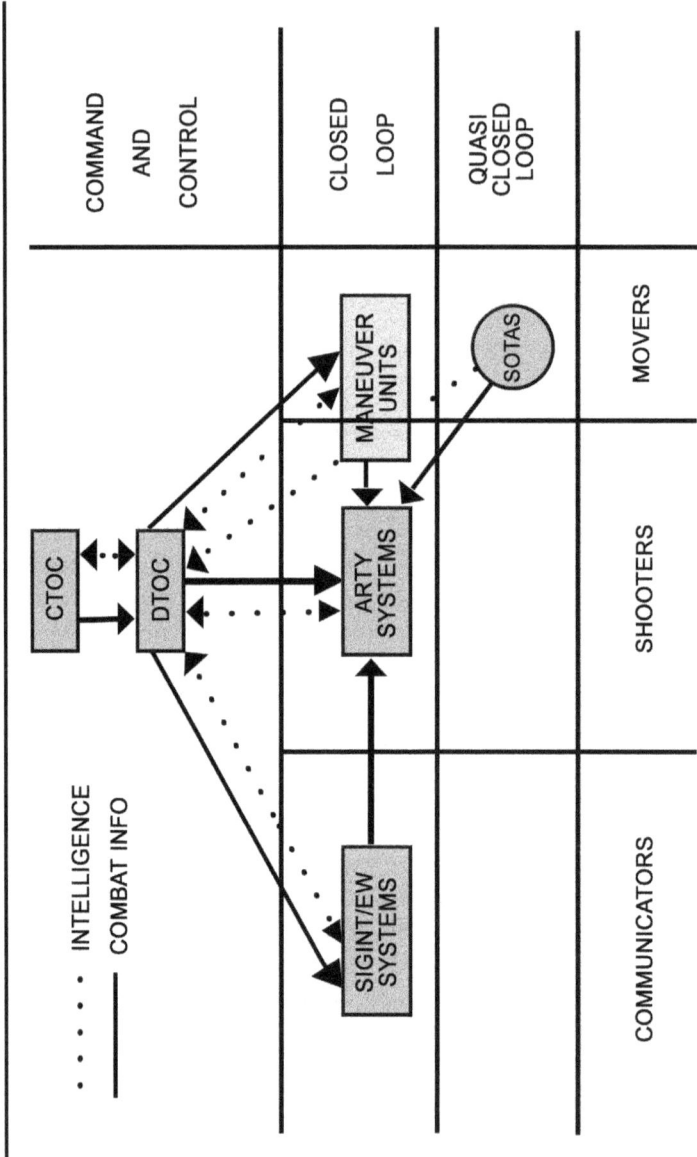

Source: Office of Battlefield Systems Integration/IBM, 1977

consisted of real-time overlays which presented accumulated locations of enemy communicators, shooters and movers as well as a large screen display of the maneuver situation (threats) with friendly unit positions.

The purpose of DIVRAS was to directly utilize combat information in real time thus improving targeting and maneuver operations at the division and below levels thus increasing force multiplication. The concept recognized the value of well analyzed but less timely intelligence products and did not replace the traditional intelligence analytical functions but was designed to complement them.

We concluded that the key features of a division automation system should include: a small division computer; a graphic display; a closed loop use of combat data; correlation and templating; and automatic data entry.

IBM utilized the aforementioned features for the division automated system as a guideline. First they developed a realistic scenario to drive real time functional requirements. The basis of the scenario was again the SCORES European situation developed by the Combined Arms Center. Specific scenarios were written to describe the flow of battle in sufficient detail for data generation. The analyses of information flow depended both upon the data content and the rules of engagement. DIVRAS applications had to be capable of supporting interfaces to the main closed loop systems indicated in Chart 29. Specific input and output message types and message rate requirements for those interfaces were determined. This large flow of data into the DTOC and other interfaces required procedures to identify and coordinate multiple messages from different sources and to provide hard target data to the various weapons systems. Therefore, improved communications were essential. The outstanding and ground breaking DIVRAS analyses performed by IBM were published in a two-volume documentation of the functional requirements[27] identified and a demonstration using a commercial ADP workshop facility was given to DOD personnel

We have discussed the basic elements for a DTOC automated coordination system which permits immediate reactions. They are: all source; near real time; formatted information; dispersed elements; multiple (distributed) access data exchange; and reduced vulnerability.

It was apparent there was a need for fundamental changes in the methods used for handling battlefield information[28]. Numerous factors were contributing to a shift from voice intensive networks to more data communications with wider information dissemination and less reliance on

Chart 29

CLOSED LOOP SYSTEMS

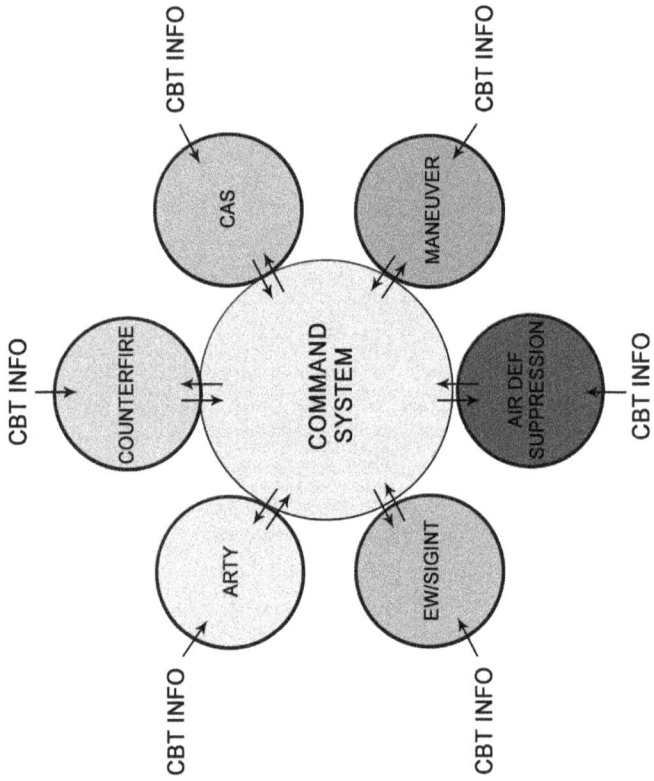

Source: Office of Battlefield Systems Integration/MITRE, 1977

voice as a primary means of information exchange. The factors influencing change included: anticipated use of an extensive complement of advanced tactical battlefield sensors to detect, identify, and track targets; the need to disseminate information laterally among several battlefield elements quickly; the need for protection from enemy electronic warfare efforts; and the potential widespread use of small, low cost data processors. Also, there was an operationally related need to improve the real time capability and accuracy of position-fixing systems used on the battlefield. At the time, two developmental systems offered a potential to meet this need; the Joint tactical Information and Distribution System (JTIDS)[29] and the Position Location and Reporting System (PLRS).

The important ongoing developments in firepower, weapons and sensors required that equivalent emphasis be placed on the development of the command and control mission area systems necessary for integration. An effective integration concept overlaid on command and control systems would greatly improve battlefield effectiveness providing a major force multiplication. Command and control must optimize enhanced target acquisition by:

- Improved Communications   (Time)
- Data Fusion   (High Value Targets.)
- Graphical Displays   (Maneuver)
- Closed Loop Targeting   (Real Time Response)
- Better Procedures   (Administration)

Since command and control overlays all the other eight mission areas it is absolutely essential that this important capability be given the highest priority if the Army is to be an effective, integrated fighting force.

MAN-MACHINE INTERFACE

As stated previously battle effectiveness depends upon the capability of weapons, the proficiency of soldiers, and the tactics and techniques of commanders

Up until now we have been discussing the importance of the integration and capabilities of weapons systems. But what about the quality and proficiency of the soldier? In 1976, 81.1% of enlisted personnel on active duty were high school graduates, over 10% greater than in 1972 under the draft. However, only 58.6% of the 180,175 new accessions that year were high school graduates[1]. After Vietnam, the propensity of sixteen to twenty-one year old males to enlist in the military was noticeably decreasing. At the time, the average reading level of Army soldiers was the 9th grade. In terms of personnel, the quality in the Army was high, however, half of new accessions were below average, there was a decreased propensity to enlist, and soldiers had poor reading skills.

In 1975, the Army was in the forefront of the largest modernization program in history, which was brought about by the rapid advancement of technology. There was much more equipment in the hands of soldiers, for example, an armored division had 11,000 major items of equipment[2]. The trend was towards complex crew serviced weapons. Repair parts were increasing, the helicopter had 12,115 and the M60-A3 had 7,260 repair parts. Not only that but there was a tremendous variety of equipment requiring 60 career fields and 389 military occupational specialties (MOS). The wheeled vehicle mechanic, for example, found 171 different makes and models of vehicles in the field.

The conclusion was that manpower skills were not improving but weapons were greatly increasing in complexity. The same situation exists in 2017. The Army was faced with the requirement to procure more advanced weapons systems that were more difficult to operate and maintain, thus mitigating against proper unit training which resulted in inefficient organizations. The situation drove MILPERCEN to suggest developing a method for "Placing limitations on weapons systems designed to assure that such systems do not exceed the availability of qualitative personnel resources of the Army." Obviously, there was a man-machine interface problem that had to be addressed. At least 33% of the personnel in the US Armed Forces were engaged in some aspect of full-time maintenance.

To solve the man-machine interface problem, the Army undertook a new approach which integrated the development of technical documentation with the development of fully-compatible performance oriented training materials, the Integrated Technical Documentation and Training (ITDT) Program. BSI spearheaded this program with TRADOC and AMC.

The basic concept underlying this approach was that the amount of resources that had to be devoted to training is tied directly to how well the documentation communicates to the soldier the information he needs to perform his tasks in the on-the-job situations.

When privates to colonels in the Army were asked, "What activities are most important to you?", they almost uniformly answered, "Individual training and maintenance." These were the areas that ITDT was designed to improve.

The end products comprising a typical ITDT package consist of two parts: Documentation and Training. The technical documentation consists of fully proceduralized job performance manuals (JPM) and job performance guides (JPG). The JPM presents all the information normally needed for moment-to-moment, on-the-job task performance. The information is organized into separate volumes by major types of tasks (operation, scheduled maintenance, troubleshooting, corrective maintenance) to facilitate on-the-job reference and use. The JPG serves both as a supplement to the JPM and as a primary training document. It contains access and enabling tasks, frequently repeated task sequences, safety and emergency procedures, and the use of basic tools and test equipment. In addition, the JPG contains representative sets of unique tasks selected from the JPM as necessary to address all skill and knowledge competencies required for the performance of the JPM-referenced tasks. Task information in both the JPM and JPG is presented in terms of detailed, illustrated, step-by-step performance sequences.

The training materials consist of extension training materials (ETM) and an associated training handbook. The training materials are used in conjunction with the JPM and JPG to teach and develop proficiency in task performance and in the efficient use of the JPM/JPG documentation. The training handbook serves as a management and administrative guide for students and supervisors. It explains how to initiate and conduct training using the lesson kits and JPG, and includes basic management instructions, record-keeping aids, and a listing or index of applicable ETM lesson kits.

One may ask "What's new? The Army already had equipment documentation and training courses." That was true, but there were many shortcomings. With respect to Documentation: it was often incomplete, pertinent information was scattered and difficult to understand, there were excessive references, a high error content, it relied on technicians' memory and it was not written to users capabilities. For example, the soldier's average grade level reading comprehension was 9th grade, yet out of 470 technical manuals reviewed only twenty-seven were written at the 9th grade or lower level. Equipment contractors were writing at their level and not to the soldiers' level, thus making the manuals difficult for soldiers to understand.

With respect to training shortcomings: courses were not rigidly tied to job requirements, it covered theory rather than task orientation, it was often given at the wrong time with too much too soon, and was not instructionally efficient nor economical.

The most important aspect of ITDT was that it is <u>task oriented</u>. A task is a identifiable and measurable unit of work. When I had staff responsibility for Army training at CONARC/TRADOC in 1972-73 we required all schools and training center courses to be system engineered for training. The system engineering approach to course design provided an orderly process of gathering and analyzing job performance requirements, of preparing and conducting training, and of evaluating and improving effectiveness. It is based on the premise that each task to be performed in a job or the behavior required of the job holder can be identified and analyzed. The first step was to perform a job analysis and develop a task list. The second step was to select tasks for training, identifying those tasks for school training and those for on-the-job training. What is greatly misunderstood by unit commanders in the field is the fact that the school training establishment does not have the time or resources to train soldiers in all of the MOS identified tasks. Tasks selected for school training were those performed by a large percentage of job holders, those performed frequently, those critical to the unit mission, and those essential in performing other critical tasks. These tasks rarely exceeded twenty-five percent of the total tasks. Consequently, the majority of identified tasks in any given MOS must be taught OJT and the relationship of training and documentation to identified tasks is a key factor. ITDT integrates the development of technical documentation with the development of fully compatible performance-oriented training materials. The basic concept of

ITDT is that resources devoted to training are tied directly to how well the documentation communicates the information that a soldier needs to perform his tasks.

The ITDT development process is summarized in Chart 30[3]. The critical areas are the front end analysis and the validation and verification procedures. The front end analysis entails a systematic process of job/task data collection, analysis, and decision making to provide the basic data and documentation/training decisions needed for developing the technical manuals and training materials. It is subdivided into three areas: equipment analysis, functional analysis, and task analysis.

A primary purpose of the equipment analysis is to identify all tasks involved in the operation and maintenance of the system. The principal product of this analysis is a task matrix which lists all tasks (operate, inspect, service, repair, etc.) actually performed on each item of equipment and the level (operator, organizational maintenance, direct support, etc.) at which it is performed.

The functional analysis defines equipment operations in terms of functional data flows and relationships among system components. Major products of this analysis are a set of functional block diagrams and associated listings of equipment failure modes, malfunction symptoms and fault isolation procedures for use in developing troubleshooting strategies and procedures.

In the task analysis step, each task is detailed in terms of task performance conditions, initiating cues, standards, and step-by-step performance procedures; analyzed in terms of behavioral performance requirements (skill, knowledge, attitudinal, informational).

ITDT requires comprehensive failure analysis which provides a soldier step-by-step procedures to troubleshoot. A major product of ITDT is the diagnostic procedures. The importance of diagnostic procedures cannot be overstated because this is the only way that we can make the important step from peacetime to wartime situations. This fundamental point bears emphasis. For example, if the water temperature gauge on a truck indicates hot, there are certain steps a driver must take. The first would be to check the fluid in the radiator. If there is no fluid and the radiator has been damaged, it makes no difference to the repair mechanic whether the radiator was damaged in peacetime by a rock thrown from the road or during wartime due to a bullet. In other words, the symptoms are invariant.

Chart 30

ITDT DEVELOPMENT PROCESS

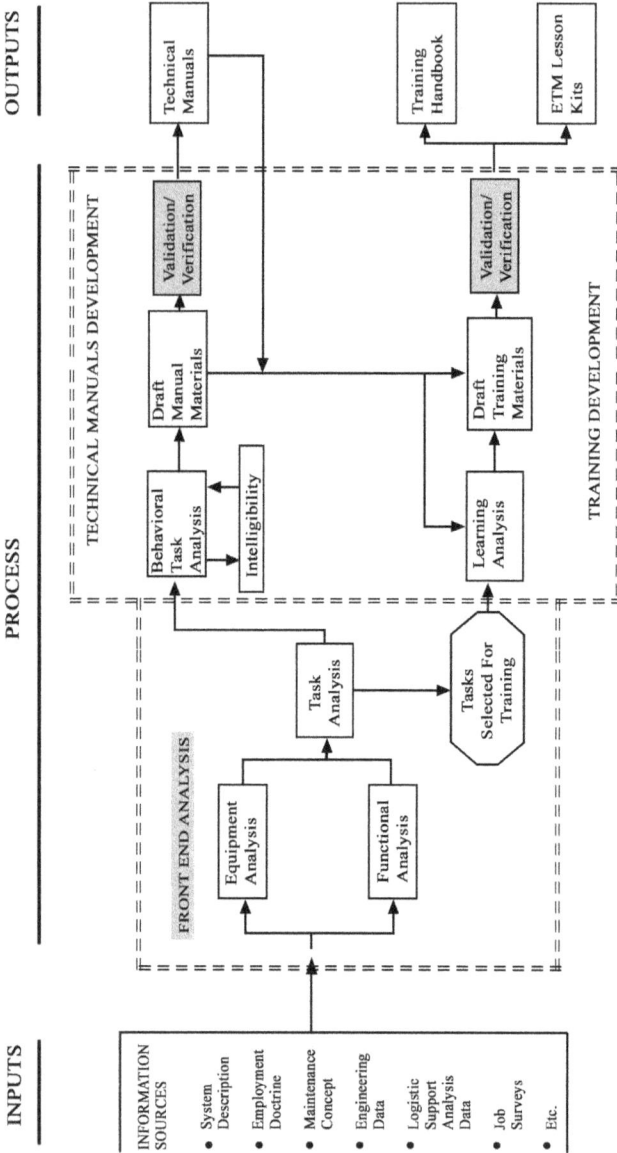

INPUTS

PROCESS

OUTPUTS

INFORMATION SOURCES

- System Description
- Employment Doctrine
- Maintenance Concept
- Engineering Data
- Logistic Support Analysis Data
- Job Surveys
- Etc.

FRONT END ANALYSIS

Equipment Analysis

Functional Analysis

Task Analysis

Tasks Selected For Training

TECHNICAL MANUALS DEVELOPMENT

Behavioral Task Analysis

Intelligibility

Draft Manual Materials

Validation/ Verification

Technical Manuals

TRAINING DEVELOPMENT

Learning Analysis

Draft Training Materials

Validation/ Verification

Training Handbook

ETM Lesson Kits

Source: Briefing. The Army's ITDT Program, 1977

152

The most important steps in the development phase of the ITDT process are the validation and verification of the technical manuals and associated training courses. The industrial contractor is required to perform a 100% validation of documented maintenance procedures on equipment with people representative of the target population. Verification has the same purpose as validation except that it is performed by the Army and not the developer contractor. Every task described in a technical manual is subjected to an acceptance trial, called verification, in which ten soldiers new to the system but skilled in common tools, test equipment, and shop procedure, try to perform the task. At least eight must complete each task successfully for the government to accept the documentation.

> Validation determines, is the content correct?
> Verification determines if solders can learn?
> Together they close the performance loop.

Various information sources are listed in Chart 30 as inputs to the front end analysis. This input data is processed in the technical manuals to include among other things Maintenance Allocation Charts which identify maintenance tasks and assign them to operators, organizational, direct support (DS) or general support (GS), maintenance and time standards which are the number of man hours required for the performance of each task.

What we're missing at the time were frequency charts showing the number of times each of the tasks would be performed annually. Current manpower authorization criteria included data provided by DARCOM of the annual man-hour requirements per system by organizational, DS, and GS maintenance. From this the Tables of Organization and Equipment were developed. At the time the way in which man-hours for maintenance was estimated was not satisfactory and studies were ongoing to improve the situation. ITDT outputs should greatly improve current data.

In the field I often pondered the fact that my mechanics always had to work overtime. In reviewing AR570-2 it was discovered that the available man hours per soldier were based on wartime work schedules, i.e., twelve hours per day, 365 days per year, and the TOEs were constructed using those inputs to determine personnel requirements. Obviously, there was a mismatch between peacetime man hours and wartime tasks assigned.

Fortunately, DARCOM already had a new equipment program for determining maintenance and supply requirements called Integrated Logistics Support (ILS). Actually, ITDT was just one of the outputs of ILS.

The so-called front end analysis was nothing more or less than putting together an ILS package and adding into it behavioral analysis. An important output of ILS, the basis upon which TOEs are determined, as well as documentation, is the Maintenance Allocation Chart, which is the only document that blends people and equipment[4].

The Patriot Missile was one of the first developmental items of equipment with design features to greatly improve maintainability. It had extensive use of build-in test equipment, fast fault isolation, the use of throw away items, a reduction of system peculiar parts, and the standardization of replaceable units. All of which led to a reduced need for personnel and equipment.

In summary in 1976 ITDT was a new and evolving concept. It embodied features which had long been recognized as desirable but which had not been attainable until recently. In particular, it integrated the development of technical documentation and training to provide a composite package of information and training directly applicable to maximizing on-the-job performance while minimizing the expenditure of supporting resources.

At the time, recognizing that the Army had experienced problems because of a lack of interoperability of its systems which were increasing in complexity and had to be efficiently operated by soldiers whose manpower skills were static, the goal of Battlefield System Integration was to provide integrated, simple effective equipment which could be easily maintained and operated by adequately trained personnel which then would insure that leaders could develop unit tactics and techniques to protect against potential threats. ITDT was an important step in both maintenance and training.

CONCLUSIONS

This book has been written to explain the pertinent steps taken by BSI in the mid-seventies to determine the most effective battlefield systems architecture for the Army which was constantly improving its combat systems, doctrine, training and techniques in hopes that the analyses taken then might be of value today in developing the army's transformation, particularly the input-output cost analysis and the method of relating technology to battlefield systems. These two steps were invaluable enabling us to focus on problem areas and to identify potential cost savings thereby optimizing combat systems development.

In 1975, the US Army was required to refocus its attention from the wars in Southeast Asia to a potential all-out major conflict in Europe, while it was undergoing the largest modernization program in its history attempting to play catch-up with the modernized Soviet military force that posed a threat to NATO in Central Europe. At that time BSI was established and directed to consider materiel, doctrinal and organizational issues in a coherent battlefield system, thereby overcoming the structural deficiencies which existed when considering combat developments by commodity commands and branch service schools functional lines. By analyzing "How the Army Fights" and adopting the DOD standard operational capabilities, technology forecasts, and threat assessments, it enabled mission capabilities to be identified and furthered the interoperability of combat systems. More importantly, it enhanced the dialogue between the user and developer.

To insure that the Army's technological programs were objective oriented we utilized the Army's science and technology objectives, which reflected the Air-Land Battle doctrine by translating mission deficiencies and capabilities into objectives, to develop a charting system that depicted the flow of information essential to making useful evaluations (Chart 4). These charts brought together for the first time a comprehensive listing of research and developmental work units in their operational content. Pacing problems were highlighted, requirements prioritized, gaps and trade-offs identified and user/developer dialogue promoted. Interestingly, we found major disconnects between the user and developer. Often there was ongoing work for which there was no requirement. Analysis of proponent user priorities indicated that less than ten percent of the developer work units were rated critical or essential. Unbelievably at the time the all important Command and Control mission area had no critical work ongoing.

Considering current formidable budgetary restraints it would be prudent to analyze the life-cycle costs of fielded military units in order to determine where funding was being expended and where cost savings might be made. In 1976 we developed a specialized costing technique which provided a clear understanding of cost relationships: high cost areas were identified, labor intensive systems determined, and secondary and tertiary costs associated with primary military activities identified. Supply, transportation and maintenance encompassed about one-third of the life-cycle costs of a typical corps, almost as much as tanks, mechanized infantry and cannon artillery. These functions are people and not capital intensive and labor saving equipment is essential to reduce personnel requirements. There is a possible highly leveraged life-cycle cost pay off. Greater attention must be given to the potential trade-offs between the procurement of equipment and its operations as well as the training of soldiers--the man-machine interface.

Success on the battlefield depends greatly upon the proficiency and spirit of soldiers. The man-machine interface can only be solved by giving special attention to the training and schooling of soldiers to include training materiels.

The Army's modernization program of the late 70's was very successful, introducing integrated combat systems which were battle tested in the Gulf War with outstanding results. The situation today, after a decade of conflict in the Middle East is very similar to that in 1975 but much more daunting. The recently announced Air-Sea Battle doctrine has not been completely delineated and consequently the Army has yet to develop fully defined roles and missions. Unlike the earlier period which concentrated on the Soviet threat in Europe, the Air-Sea Battle doctrine is not focused on any one country, although the current Chinese military buildup is a matter of concern, and Asia appears to be an area of prime interest, thereby requiring the analysis of the military capabilities of several nations. Not only that, today the Army finds itself with aging and worn-out equipment and a legacy of recent procurement programs in disarray while facing drastic reductions in funding.

Technology continues to provide improved sensors, high speed processing, and distributed communications while offering real time target acquisition and command and control which requires enhanced battlefield systems management. Currently the Army's high priority modernization programs include the development of several important ISTA and command and control systems such as the Warfighter Information Network, the Joint Tactical Radio System, and the Distributed Common Ground System. These state of the art systems will be absolutely essential in the total spectrum conflicts since they enable our forces to obtain favorable combat force ratios by taking advantage of force multiplication. Dynamic force management requires flexible, fast, precise information processing. Considering the newly enunciated Air-Sea Battle doctrine, changes required by revised policies, doctrines and organizations will be endemic to command and control. Therefore flexible command and control test beds will be absolutely essential to determine the most logical solutions. Technology is increasing at a rapid rate, so that rather than concentrating on hardware, which many developers are prone to do, stress should be placed on procedures if successful systems are to be fielded. With respect to tactical data systems in the seventies we found that hardware was not the problem; software was often late, costly, and non-responsive. Requirements change and change must be part of the plan.

Although industry and military developers generally focus on creating new and more lethal combat systems, considering the reduced funding situation it might prudent to focus on the "now" problems by incrementally improving current systems. Product improvement is less costly and often very effective. The incremental value of improvements to increase a weapon's effectiveness can be obtained by utilizing linear equations to arrive at an optimal solution. However, to determine the relative value of one combat system to others so that meaningful trade-offs between systems can be considered, heterogeneous dynamic modeling is required. Only then can the most effective integrated force structure be arrived at.

Material acquisition is a very complex endeavor and requires the coordination of many different organizations. Rarely does it proceed effortlessly and normally there are minor and often times major glitches. During the mid-seventies some senior personnel were very concerned about the overall effectiveness of the Army's developmental processes. One of these individuals was General John R. Deane, Jr., the Commanding General of the Army Materiel Command. Recognizing BSI's ability to look at the Army's weapons systems in the context of a total system and to participate in current combat development/materiel acquisition activities enabled it to discern shortcomings in the materiel development process, he asked me to provide my thoughts at the time on materiel development. They coincided remarkably with his, and in August 1977 they were briefed to General Bernard W. Rogers, the Army Chief of Staff. Perhaps these

Jrmentenvironment.gationmentperceived shortcomings of yesteryear might even be pertinent in today's materiel acquisition environment.

Thoughts on Materiel Development

Two years ago, I was given the mission of reviewing Army systems in close coordination with the User in order to integrate the battlefield. This was to be accomplished by conducting systems studies, examining for inter operability, identifying gaps, eliminating duplication, participating in evaluations and monitoring programs. We early realized that two factors, enhanced intelligence and target acquisition and increased battle tempo, are dramatically changing the equations of warfare. Considering the dynamics of change in both technology and tactics, we have suggested improvements in materiel acquisition which generally have encountered road blocks of the following nature:

1. Doctrine. Often not available in timely manner to evaluate or integrate new weapons systems.
2. Long Range Orientation. Not enough emphasis on the "NOW" problems facing commanders in the field.
3. State-of-the-Art Developments. Development centers and industry both push revolutionary in precedence over evolutionary developments.
4. Product Improvements. The emphasis on long range revolutionary developments mitigates against PI. Need strong DA policy to implement this cost effective method of improving battlefield capabilities.
5. Threat. Not enough concentration on enemy capabilities. Soviets always appear to be ten feet tall when they have exploitable weaknesses.
6. Means not Ends. There is a preoccupation with prerogatives and not enough focus on substance.
7. Data. Insufficient data available on costs and relative combat effectiveness to enhance decision making.
8. Studies. Studies often optimize systems being considered. Weak points come out later and are expensive to fix.

158

9. Not invented here. The NIH syndrome is
    prevalent and will do much to inhibit NATO
    standardization efforts.
10. Don't rock the boat. This syndrome permeates.
    Am continuously told that such and such an idea
    could jeopardize ongoing programs. The Army
    should want the most cost effective solution.
11. Field experiments. There is a reluctance to
    conduct field experiments to smoke out
    potential problems early.
12. Test beds. Although enunciated policy, not
    sufficiently implemented.
13. R&D Focus. Needs to be more oriented on
    requirements. SPIDER CHARTS and STOG are steps
    in the right direction but need aggressive
    follow through.
14. Selling the Army Position. It is perceived
    that the Army's requirements are not fully
    understood by OSD/Congress. Believe that a
    mission area systems approach could improve our
    ability to tell our story.

Then and probably more than ever today, a systems approach to materiel development is essential. It is necessary to have a defined architecture synergizing the development of forces, materiel and technology. Today's transformation which proposes to link combat platforms to sensors is a giant step in the right direction. It will provide a much needed network of manned and unmanned vehicles, intelligence sensors, communications and combat systems. To accomplish this major task the proper choice of technology is crucial...and very difficult. Recently, for example, the future Combat System has been terminated and the important Joint Tactical Radio System wideband network has technological problems. Unfortunately, difficulties will always exist when developmental programs are pushing the state-of-the-art. It is believed that the transformational efforts of the 70's will be of assistance today in producing new system concepts and initiating developments which treat the Army in the field as a total cohesive system, integrated so that combat systems, including appropriate components of the US Air Force and the Navy are configured to operate in a common architecture which will maximize the total system capabilities, supporting the Air-Sea Battle doctrine.

BIBLIOGRAPHY

1.1   Campaign Summaries, 1944, Department of Military Art and Engineering, US Military Academy, West Point, NY

1.2   John MacDonald, Great Battlefields of the World, 1985, Macmillan Publishing Co, New York

1.3   Great Captains before Napoleon, 1944, Department of Military Art and Engineering, US Military Academy, West Point, NY

1.4   Supplemental Material on the First World War, Department of Military Art and Engineering, US Military Academy, 1944, West Point, NY

1.5   MG Hunt, Ira A., 9th Infantry Division in Vietnam, Unequaled and Unparalleled, 2010, The University Press of Kentucky, Lexington, KY

1.6   Kramer, John W., Informal Presentation Paper, Some Incomplete Data on the 5734-5735 War, 21Jan74, US Material Systems Analysis Agency, Aberdeen Proving Ground, Maryland

2.1   Wakelin, James H., Letter to Commander, US Army Materiel Command, No date, Alexandria, VA

2.2   Deputy Assistant Secretary of the Army, Poor, Charles L., Letter to Secretary of the Army, 31Dec1974, Washington, DC

2.3   Secretary of the Army, Calloway, Bo, Memorandum for the Under Secretary of the Army, 1May1975, Secretary of the Army, Washington, DC

2.4   Emerson, K.C., Memorandum, Subj: Reprogramming of FCRC Ceiling, 25Nov1975, Office of Assistant Secretary, DA, Washington, DC

3.1   Letter, Subj: Initiatives in the Technology Base, 29Oct1975, ODCSOPS, DA, Washington, DC

5.1   MG Hunt, Ira A., Unpublished doctoral thesis, Military Contributions to United States Economic Growth, 1964, The George Washington University, Washington, DC

5.2   Study, Subj: Input-Output Analysis, 1976, Battlefield Systems Integration DARCOM, Alexandria, VA

6.1   Senator Sam Nunn and Senator Dewey Bartlett, NATO and the New Soviet Threat, 24Jan1977, Report to the Senate

Armed Services Committee, US Congress, Washington, DC

6.2   Understanding Soviet Military Developments, Apr77, AST-1100S-100-77, OACSI, DA, Washington, DC

6.3   Col. Konyushenko, I, "Meeting Engagement", Red Star, 17Mar1976

6.4   LTC Bubnov, O and Lt. Kharitonov, Paper, Subj: Ruler for Calculating Smoke Screens, Military Herald, No. 1, 1975

6.5   Karber, Philip A, "The Soviet Anti-Tank Debate", Current News, Special Edition, No. 131, 17Aug1976, Dept. of Air Force

6.6   Braddock, J. V. and Wikner, NF, An Assessment of Soviet Forces Facing NATO – The Central Region and Suggested NATO Initiatives, Draft Copy, 1976, BDM Corp., Washington, DC

6.7   Col. Sidorenko, AA, The Offensive, a Glimpse of Modern Soviet Artillery Tactics, Field Artillery Journal 42:32-45, July-August 1974

6.8   Military Operations of the Soviet Army, 23May1976, US Army Intelligence Threat Analysis Detachment, OACSI, DA, Washington, DC

6.9   DePuy, WE, Letter, Subj: Formal Meeting with the Germans, 7Apr77, CG TRADOC, Ft. Monroe, VA

7.1   Report, Subj: Executive Summary; Limited Visibility Operations Assessment, Jan1977. Harry Diamond Laboratories, Adelphi, MD

7.2   Boyd, David; Byrne, Peter; Penrod, Darrell, Series of Reports, Zone II Interdiction Study, 1977, MITRE/METREK Corp, McLean, VA

7.3   Col. Sidorenko, AA, The Offensive, a Glimpse of Modern Soviet Artillery Tactics, Field Artillery Journal 42:32-45, July-August 1974

8.1   MG Hunt, Ira A., Memorandum, Subj: Are the Army's Procurement Priorities Sound?, 17Mar76, Hq. AMC, Alexandria, VA

8.2   Paper, Subj: Army "Top40" Procurement Priority List, 26Feb1976, Ch. Requirements Program Div., ODCOPS, DA, Washington, DC

9.1   Kramer, John W., Informal Presentation Paper, Subj: Some Iincomplete Data on the 5734-5735 War, 21Jan74, US

Material Systems Analysis Agency, Aberdeen Proving
Ground, MD

9.2   Karber, Philip A., "The Soviet Anti-Tank Debate", Current
        News, Special Edition, No131, 17Aug1976, Dept. of Air
        Force

9.3   Marshal Grechko AA, Armed Forces of the Soiviet State, 2nd
        Ed., Moscow, 1975

9.4   Kramer, John W, Presentation Paper, Subj: Survivability,
        5Nov1974, US Army Materiel Systems Analysis Activity,
        Aberdeen Proving Grounds, MD

9.5   MG Hunt, Ira A., Memorandum, Subj: Ineffectiveness of
        Copperhead in Line-of-Sight Battle, 9Dec77, Hq, Army
        Materiel Command, Alexandria, VA

9.6   Col. Shaporalov, N, Article, Subj: Teaching Crews to
        Combat Tanks, Self-propelled Artillery and ATGM, Military
        Herald, No. 6, Jun1975

9.7   Koritchuck, "The Struggle with Anti-Tank Means in the
        Offensive", Military Herald, June 1975

9.8   Brady E. and Famolari E., Supplement to the ISTA Mission
        Area Review: Exploring ISTA Contributions to Tactical
        Actions at Division Level and Below, March 1977, METREK
        Div., MITRE Corp., McLean, VA

9.9   Yondorf, Walter F., Letter, Subj: Inputs to Sensor
        Effectiveness Model, 25Feb77, MITRE Corp., McLean, VA

9.10   Oldham, Max S., Internal Memorandum, Subj: Developing
        Intelligence Target Relative Values, 9Mar77, MITRE Corp.,
        Alexandria, VA

9.11   Briefing Charts, Sensor Effectiveness, 1977, MITRE Corp.,
        Alexandria, VA

9.12   Tidwell, W.A., Working Paper, Factors Degrading Sensor
        System Performance, 3Jan77, MITRE Corp., McLean, VA

9.13   Study, Review of the ISTA Mission Area, (Major Findings
        and Key Issues), 1976, METREK Div., MITRE Corp.,
        McLean, VA

9.14   Brady, E. and Famolari, E., Study Subj: Exploring ISTA
        Contributions to Tactical Actions at Division Level and
        Below, 26May1977, MTR-7497, MITRE Corp., McLean, VA

9.15   Brady E., & Famolari E., Owens F., Supplement to ISTA
        Mission Are Review: The Integration of ISTA Systems with

Army Command and Control Structure, March 1977, MTR-7508, METREK Div., MITRE Corp., McLean, VA

9.16 Study, Subj: Reconnaissance, Surveillance and Target Acquisition (RSTA) Functional Study, Oct1976, MITRE Corp., McLean, VA

9.17 Dr. Malcomb R. Currie, Director of Defense Research and Engineering Statement before House Armed Services Committee, 94th Congress, 1st Session, 21Feb1975, Washington, DC

9.18 Kroger, M.G., Paper, Subj: Command vs. Control, Oct1976, Submitted to Director of Battlefield Systems Integration

9.19 Tidwell, W.A., Study, Subj: A Concept for the Corps Operations Command Complex in the 1980's (M76-33), July1976, MITRE Corp., McLean, VA

9.20 Report to Director of Battlefield Systems Integration, Subj: Command and Control Functions, June1977, MITRE Corp., McLean, VA

9.21 Work Submittal, Plan for the Development of an Army Target Acquisition Capability (ATACG), 1976, MITRE Corp., McLean, VA

9.22 Working Paper, Command and Control Functions, 1977, DBSI, DARCOM, Alexandria, VA

9.23 Gen. William Westmoreland, Article Prepared for NY Times, 1976

9.24 MG Hunt, Ira A., Letter, Subj: Areas of Concern in Command and Control, 20May77, DBSI, DARCOM, Alexandria, VA

9.25 Point Paper, Subj: USAREUR's Highest Priority Material Needs, 23Aug76, DCSOPS, Hq. USAREUR and Seventh Army, Germany

9.26 Draft Report, Subj: Division Real Time Applications Report, 3June77, Fed. Systems Div., IBM, Arlington, VA (Methodology)

9.27 Report, Subj: Division Real Time Applications Report, 3Aug77, Federal Systems Div., IBM, Arlington, VA (Software Functional Description)

9.28 Study, Battlefield Surveillance and Communication Interoperability, July 1977, METREK Div., MITRE(M77-81), McLean, VA

9.29   MG Hunt, Ira A., Memorandum, Subj: <u>Status of JTIDS Class III Terminal Development</u>, 30Aug76, DBSI, DARCOM, Alexandria, VA

10.1   Information Paper, Subj: <u>Mental Categories</u>, 16June1976, DAPE-MPE-CS, DA, Washington DC

10.2   Briefing Charts, Subj: <u>What about the type of equipment?</u>, 1977, DBSI, DARCOM, Alexandria, VA

10.3   Briefing, <u>The Army's ITDT Program</u>, 1977, DARCOM/TRADOC 1TDT Committee, Washington, DC

10.4   MG Hunt, Ira A., Memorandum, Subj: <u>Integrated Technical Documentation Training (ITDT)</u>, 23Dec1977, DBSI, DARCOM, Alexandria, VA

ABOUT THE AUTHOR

MG(Ret) Ira A. Hunt Jr. is a 1945 graduate of the U.S. Military Academy. He later taught at both West Point and the Naval Academy. Returning to troop duty in Germany his battalion soldiers set a European tank gunnery qualification record. In 1966 he was assigned to the Office of the Secretary of Defense where he was the action officer for the relocation of America troops in Europe, an exercise that Secretary McNamara cited as his most satisfactory accomplishment. In the Vietnam conflict he was both Chief of Staff and a Brigade Commander in the 9th Infantry Division where his troops called him "Rice Paddy Daddy". Subsequently, he had staff responsibility for the operations of the Army's Schools and Training Centers. He returned to Southeast Asia as Deputy Commander, USSAG overseeing the wars in South Vietnam and Cambodia and the evacuations of Phnom Penh and Saigon. His last assignment prior to retiring in 1978 was as Director of Battlefield Systems Integration.

General Hunt's awards and decorations include: The Distinguished Service Medal with OLC; Silver Star with OLC; Legion of Merit with 3 OLCs; Distinguished Flying Cross; Soldiers Medal; Bronze Star Medal with 3 OLCs, one with V Device; Air Medal with 14 OLCs; Army Commendation Medal with OLC; Purple Heart with OLC; Combat Infantry Badge; Parachutist Badge, and Foreign Decorations